IMPROVING URBAN SCHOOLS

Education in an Urbanised Society

Education continues to face a range of problems, crises, issues and challenges. Often, although not exclusively, those experiencing the most severe problems are working within an urban context. Such schools face very particular challenges – high ethnic minority intake, pupil underachievement, problems of teacher recruitment and retention, social deprivation and other factors. Teachers themselves need to be prepared for classes with a rapid turnover of pupils, pupils from homeless and refugee families, pupils with English as an additional language.

This series is intended to help education professionals and academics gain a broader understanding of the challenges faced. It will examine the problems facing teachers and learners working in challenging and difficult circumstances, with a view to overcoming disadvantage in contemporary education in the UK and Ireland. It will explore social and educational developments and will provide educational practitioners, academics and policy makers with focused analyses of key issues facing schools in an urban society, examining the interaction between theory and practice. It will offer insights into the linkage between education development and wider social, cultural and economic needs and thus contribute to the achievement of social justice in and through education.

Jill Rutter: *Refugees Children in the UK*

Meg Maguire, Tim Woodridge & Simon Pratt-Adams: *The Urban Primary School*

Pat Broadhead & Chrissy Meleady: *Children Families & Communities*

Mel Ainscow & Mel West: *Improving Urban Schools*

IMPROVING URBAN SCHOOLS

LEADERSHIP AND COLLABORATION

Edited by

MEL AINSCOW AND MEL WEST

Open University Press

Open University Press
McGraw-Hill Education
McGraw-Hill House
Shoppenhangers Road
Maidenhead
Berkshire
England
SL6 2QL

email: enquiries@openup.co.uk
world wide web: www.openup.co.uk

and Two Penn Plaza, New York, NY 10121–2289, USA

First published 2006

A catalogue record of this book is available from the British Library

ISBN 10: 0335 21911 X (pb) 0 335 21912 8 (hb)
ISBN 13: 9780335219117 (pb) 9780335219124 (hb)

Library of Congress Cataloging-in-Publication Data
CIP data applied for

Typeset by YHT Ltd, London
Printed in Poland by OZ Graf. S.A.
www.polskabook.pl

CONTENTS

NOTES ON CONTRIBUTORS

Mel Ainscow is Professor of Education and Co-director of the Centre for Equity in Education at the University of Manchester. Previously a headteacher, local education authority inspector and lecturer at the University of Cambridge, his work attempts to explore connections between inclusion, teacher development and school improvement. Mel is Co-director of the school improvement network, Improving the Quality of Education for All (IQEA); Consultant to UNESCO, UNICEF and Save the Children; and Marden Visiting Professor at the Hong Kong Institute of Education.

Alan Dyson is Professor of Education and Co-director of the Centre for Equity in Education at the University of Manchester. His work is concerned with urban education, inclusion, school–community interactions and with the relationship between them. He has worked in universities since 1988, prior to which he taught for 13 years, mainly in urban comprehensive schools.

Samantha Fox has worked on several projects including a three year project on leadership, behaviour and learning with Mel Ainscow. Her main research interests are in the field of inclusion, school improvement and the management of change, particularly in the urban context. More recently she has co-authored a school self-review instrument in partnership with a local education authority that evaluates inclusion using pupil voice as a principal means of data collection.

Helen Gunter is Professor of Educational Policy, Leadership and Management in the School of Education at the University of Manchester. She has published widely on the theory and practice of educational leadership. Her research interests are mainly located in knowledge production in the field of educational leadership, with a particular focus on how personal narratives and artifacts enable understandings to be generated about identity and practice.

Andy Howes is a lecturer on teacher training and research methodology courses in the School of Education at the University of Manchester. His work is focused on teacher development and the effects of schooling on individuals and communities, particularly at the secondary level. He has taught science in Oxford, Indonesia and London.

Andrew Morley is an education consultant currently working with schools in urban settings. Previously he was a headteacher working in inner-city primary schools, and it was during this time that he started his EdD at the University of Manchester, which explored the sustainable improvement of failing primary schools.

Maria Nicolaidou is currently working as a primary school teacher in Lemesos, Cyprus. Dr Nicolaidou has worked as a research associate at the Management and Institutional Development Centre, and the Educational Support and Inclusion Centre, at the School of Education, University of Manchester on a number of projects. Her main research interests lie in the broader area of school improvement and school leadership.

Jacqui Stanford continues research into urban education, collaboration and school improvement, with particular interest in the accommodation of cultural differences within schools and society. She has recently completed work for the DfES on their Excellence in Cities and the Leadership Incentive Grant policy initiatives.

Dave Tweddle was a teacher, educational psychologist and adviser/inspector for special educational needs (SEN) before becoming a senior officer in a Greater Manchester local authority. Most recently, he has worked as an independent consultant to local authorities, and collaborated with colleagues at the University of Manchester, on a wide range of SEN and inclusion issues.

Mel West joined the University of Manchester as Professor of Educational Leadership in January 2000 – a post held jointly within the Faculty of Education and the Manchester Business School. His work, principally being in the fields of school management and school improvement, has taken him to many countries including Iceland, Laos, Chile, Hong Kong, China, Puerto Rico and Malawi, working with a number of international agencies including the British Council, DfID, OECD, UNESCO and Save the Children. In the late-1980s he was one of the architects of the influential Improving the Quality of Education for All (IQEA) programme.

SERIES PREFACE

The Open University Press has been the leading publisher of urban education studies in this country. With early texts such as *Cities, Communities and the Young: Readings in Urban Education* (1973a) and *Equality and City Schools: Readings in Urban Education* (1973b), the Press gave a considerable impetus to urban education study, research and policy discussion in Britain.

This publication initiative was taken because it was recognised that teaching and learning in urban schools constituted distinctive challenges which required close analysis and imaginative and radical responses. It was also recognised that educational and social policy aspirations for equality of opportunity, social justice and community regeneration faced their greatest tests in the context of urban schooling in major cities and in large working class estates on the margins of such cities.

In England, the Department of Education and Skills publications, *The London Challenge* (2003) and *London Schools; Rising to the Challenge* (2005) demonstrate that teaching and learning in urban contexts are still high on the policy agenda. While the particular focus upon London has current priority, similar reports could be produced for Birmingham, Glasgow, Liverpool, Manchester, Belfast, Cardiff, Newcastle and other major centres. The urban education question has continuing relevance for policy and practice and it involves national and international dimensions.

It was for these reasons that we suggested to the Open University Press/ McGraw-Hill publishing team that a new series on teaching and learning in urban contexts would be very timely and professionally valuable. We were pleased that this proposal received such a positive response, not only from the publishers but also from our colleagues who will be the contributors to the series.

The series is designed to be a resource for:

• students undertaking initial teacher education

- students following programmes of Educational Studies
- serving teachers and headteachers undertaking advanced courses of study and professional development such as NPQH
- education policy professionals and administrators
- citizens who want to be actively involved in the improvement of educational services such as parents and school governors

The challenge we have set for the contributors to the series is to write texts that will engage with these various constituencies. To do this, we believe that such texts must locate the issue under examination in an appropriate theoretical, historical and cultural context; report relevant research studies; adopt a mode of analysis expected from 'reflective practitioners' – and keep all of this grounded in the realities of urban professional experience and work settings, expressed in an accessible style.

Gerald Grace, Ian Menter and Meg Maguire

EDITORS PREFACE

Urban schools have historically been regarded as posing a series of problems for those who manage them, for those who teach in them and for those who attend them. In consequence, these problematic urban schools have frequently been the subject of a range of sometimes limited and sometimes counter-productive policy initiatives. Currently in the UK setting, all schools have been subjected to the reforming drive of a national system of inspections. The consequences have been that many urban schools have been designated as 'failing' in relation to the government's intention to raise standards.

In this collection, a number of contributors have come together to explore some alternative ways forward. This book sets out to explore some of the dilemmas that surround the urban school in the English context, although it does draw on research evidence from urban settings elsewhere, particularly from the USA. All the contributors to this series take a common approach towards urban schools. As they argue in the introduction to this collection, 'we refer to schools that are mostly located in declining inner-city and sub-urban areas, and where the population is drawn from the poorest and least advantaged sections of the community'. The contributors argue that neo-liberal inspired reforms combined with a growth in economic polarisation in the UK have worked together to compound the marginalisation of some urban learners as well as widening the attainment gap. Thus, in this book, the impact of the wider social context, of what happens 'beyond the school gates' is attended to in a serious and scholarly manner.

'Improving Urban Schools' provides a thorough account of the policy background that frames the urban school. As with much research elsewhere, the contributors acknowledge the powerful impact that positive and enabling leadership can make to an individual school. As they also recognise, the 'trick' is to bring off a form of democratic leadership in challenging material circumstances and in a policy environment that contradicts the ethics and values of reciprocity. This book challenges any easy recipes for improving urban schools and argues for a contextually sensitive and democratic way forward in order to support and sustain improvements in urban schools. The book is grounded in the voices of practitioners and includes some excellent accounts of relative progress.

We have been extremely fortunate in being able to include such an original and challenging collection in this series produced, as it is, by leading experts in the field of critical leadership and school improvement studies. 'Improving Urban Schools' will provide a challenging yet inspirational corrective to some of the de-contextualised accounts of leadership and improvement. The collection takes a properly realistic approach towards urban education reform but provides accounts that eschew fatalism. Through a focus on issues such as risk and resilience, collaboration and local democratic accountability, the book conveys a sense of 'complex hope' that will inspire and encourage all those who seek to support and sustain improvement in urban schools wherever they are located.

Meg Maguire

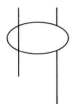

PREFACE

The term 'urban schools' may be unfamiliar to some readers. In some countries, including our own, it is not a descriptor that has yet come into general use. It is not that the particular problems or environments have not been recognized: usually they have, and there have been policy initiatives that have targeted precisely the kind of schools that feature in the studies we report. Outside the education sector, too, there is parallel recognition of the phenomenon, with initiatives taken to simulate urban or neighbourhood renewal. Despite all of this, we do not seem to have settled on common terms to describe either the contexts or the schools.

However, there is a literature addressing the problems faced by such schools that goes back at least 20 years in the USA, and is developing rapidly in a number of other English-speaking countries. Most often, this literature uses the term 'urban education'. So, while we are mindful that there are a variety of alternatives in use, and of the point made so cogently by our colleague, Alan Dyson, that there are many schools in the leafier glades of surburbia that might also be described as being urban, we feel that this is the best single descriptor for our purposes.

Briefly, then, by urban schools we mean more than simply those that are situated in urban environments. We refer to schools that are mostly located in declining inner-city and suburban areas, and where the population is drawn from the poorest and least advantaged sections of the community. We mean those schools where parental income and employment levels are low, where the national populations of ethnic and social minority groups are over-represented, and where there are sometimes significant numbers of bilingual learners. It is these schools, their teachers, their students and their communities we have in mind, and it is the work of these schools and the challenges they face that form the basis for the studies and analyses gathered together in this book.

The ideas we present arise from the involvement of the various authors with practitioners in the field. Indeed, without their inspiration, commitment and support the book would not have been possible. In this respect we must pay particular thanks to the following colleagues, all of whom have outstanding records of improving urban schools: Jan Atkinson, Stephen Ball, Yvonne Birch, Phil Doyle, Dame Jean Else, Ann Frances, John Hull, Sir John Jones, David Kershaw, Keith McDonald, Barry Morrison, Sylvia Moore, Gerard Moran and Susan Orlik. We also want to thank Averil Gould who helped to coordinate many of the projects reported in the text. Last, and by no means least, we must acknowledge Tim Brighouse and David Hargreaves, from whom we have taken immense inspiration.

Mel Ainscow and Mel West

THE CHALLENGE OF URBAN SCHOOL IMPROVEMENT

Mel West and Mel Ainscow

This introductory chapter outlines the challenges of urban education and explains the overall agenda that guided the work of the authors. It provides a brief overview of international literature on school improvement in economically disadvantaged areas before going on to explain the significance of England, where there has been intensive efforts to 'raise standards' in urban schools. The rationale behind these reform efforts is outlined, emphasizing the overall policy context of competition and choice. There is a specific focus on the role of leadership, making reference to a recent analysis of current thinking as reflected in literature from both educational and business contexts.

In his monograph on the need to reshape urban education in the USA, Peterson (1994) sets out some of the challenges facing schools. He reminds us that

> Often, they are part of a large, centralised bureaucracy that may be slow to respond to the needs of the schools. Resources are scarce, and many buildings are in disrepair. The external context may include gang activity, widespread availability and use of drugs, and a breakdown of the local community structure. Students come to school carrying the burdens of poverty, hunger and poor housing. These conditions are the realities of urban classrooms.

These are challenges that have become all too familiar to those working in schools in urban contexts in many countries. However, the emphasis on 'market led' reforms and the unleashing of competition between schools as a strategy for improvement have concentrated and accelerated the challenges in recent years (Thrupp 2001a; Giroux and Schmidt 2004). Among those left behind in the drive to raise standards are student groups (and sometimes whole schools) that have been unable to 'compete'. As Young and Melnick (1988) observe, the impact of poverty and its attendant problems tends to be more severe in inner-city environments than in other geographical settings, and this exacerbates the educational disadvantages experienced by the young people who live there. The consequence – recent modest improvements notwithstanding – is a widening of the attainment gap and increased marginalization or indeed exclusion of some groups of learners (Giroux and Schmidt 2004).

Yet, as Peterson (1994) also reminds us, the need to ensure that schools in difficult, urban contexts can effectively serve their students is paramount. If we fail to serve these children within school, we leave them to make their own way in what are often hostile and unsupportive environments outside the school. The consequences for both the children themselves and the social cohesion of urban communities, are predictable. As Golba (1998) points out, unless we find ways to reduce the inequalities in educational quality and experience available to children, they themselves will continue to be 'victims of the divisions of race and class', while neglect of this issue threatens the economic and social well-being of our communities.

At the same time, we need to be sensitive to the complexities of the environments that come to mind when we talk of urban education. Here the comments of David Hargreaves (2003c) regarding recent educational developments in London are a useful reference point. Drawing on what he describes as the classic book, *The Death and Life of Great American Cities*, written in the early 1960s by Jane Jacobs, he reminds us that some urban contexts, particularly large cities, are characterized by social and cultural diversity that has enormous potential for promoting innovation. He argues, cities tend to attract creative people whose energy and resources have to be mobilized to support educational improvement efforts.

Bearing this complexity in mind, then, this introductory chapter summarizes what we see as the current challenges confronting urban education. It provides a brief, critical overview of key international literature on school improvement in economically disadvantaged areas, before going on to explain the situation in England where there have been intensive efforts to 'raise standards' in urban schools through various national initiatives such as Excellence in Cities, Education Action Zones, foundation schools, city academies and the Leadership Incentive Grant. The rationale behind these reform efforts is discussed, emphasizing the overall policy context which embraces both competition and choice.

Improving schools in urban contexts

Recently, the Australian scholar, Roger Slee, referred to Edward Said's explanation of how, when ideas 'travel' to other times and situations, they can lose some of their 'original power and rebelliousness' (Slee 2004). This is a description that may cause some embarrassment to the school effectiveness and school improvement communities. At their point of origin, these movements were rooted in rebellion against conventional explanations about educational failure, particularly those put forward to 'explain' low educational performance in urban contexts that are characterized by poverty and deprivation (Edmonds 1979). Indeed, central to the development of these traditions is the conviction that schools can and should 'make a difference', regardless of social context. More recently, these traditions have become 'domesticated' within a political discourse that stifles discussion and equates achievement with measurable outcomes from standardized tests (Slee et al. 1998; Thrupp 1999). As a result, in national contexts such as our own where reform policies have been based on a rather narrow view of school effectiveness, strategies seeking to bring about school improvement can, in practice, act as a barrier to the development of educational practices that serve all students, particularly those in more unfavourable socioeconomic contexts.

Before the mid-1990s, researchers showed very little direct interest in schools facing difficult circumstances. School improvement researchers tended to work with organizations that already had a track record of successful innovation (Hopkins et al. 1994). Similarly, most school effectiveness research was focused upon successful schools, leading to a deficit explanation of those that were less successful – that is, they were not succeeding because they lacked the 'characteristics' of their more effective cousins (Reynolds 1991). More recently, there has been a recognition that the 'backward mapping' of such characteristics into less effective schools may be neither appropriate nor helpful (see, for example, Reynolds et al. 1996).

However, some researchers have focused on schools that are seen to be struggling, in order to find ways of helping to restore these schools to health (e.g. Louis and Miles 1990; Barber 1998; Myers and Goldstein 1998; Elmore 2000; Muijs et al. 2004). Close to the themes of this book, Harris and Chapman (2002) looked specifically at leadership practice in English secondary schools facing challenging circumstances. Reporting their study of ten such schools, they draw attention to the need to manage tensions and problems related to particular circumstances and contexts. Arguing that the main task of those in leadership positions is to cope with 'unpredictability, conflict and dissent ... without discarding core values', their work underlines the fundamental importance of matching improvement strategy to context.

In England, a key strategy for addressing the problems of schools that are a cause for concern, many of which are in difficult urban contexts, has been through the national inspection system introduced in 1992. This requires that those schools that are judged as failing to provide an acceptable standard of education be made subject to 'special measures'. The introduction of the inspection system triggered much debate about how best to deal with the problems of ineffective and failing schools (e.g. Reynolds 1995; Barber 1998). Gray (1999) suggests that, above all, such schools need to 'rediscover a sense of purpose'. This is more likely to be accomplished, he argues, if changes can be effected in three areas: commitment levels, staffing and context. While the first two are, to varying degrees, within the direct sphere of influence of the school, the contextual factors describe precisely those intransigent problems that beset schools facing challenging circumstances. There is, we suggest, a need for a much closer understanding of how actions taken by or within a school can alter or offset those contextual factors that will, otherwise, undermine clarity of purpose and limit the impact of improvements in classroom practice.

In addressing this issue, we draw on evidence from the USA, where there has been a long-term interest in schools in disadvantaged environments, and where there are a number of studies offering analyses of the particular problems faced by inner-city schools and advice on what 'makes the difference'. For example, Cotton (1991) focuses on the special problems of ethnic minority groups, but her findings – which include progress tracking, attention to tutoring as well as teaching, appropriate instructional strategies and meaningful parental involvement – would seem to have relevance for all students in difficult urban schools. Stringfield and his colleagues (1997) conducted a longitudinal study of ten school improvement 'designs' focused on improving academic achievement among poor and minority students. They reported a litany of problems, both internal and external, including low levels of teacher morale and commitment, a mismatch between the schools' curricula and the pupils' interests and aptitudes, poor leadership quality and fragmented school cultures. The image of the school was often weak, making it hard to recruit and retain both staff and pupils. A similar exercise by Ascher (1993) focused on three popular improvement programmes (the School Development Program, Accelerated Schools and Success for All), again highlighted the importance of parental participation, but also makes some interesting observations on the limitations of traditional assessment measures, while acknowledging that it would be impossible to dispense with these altogether.

Cawelti (1999) analyses accounts of schools that demonstrated a capacity to achieve unusually high levels of success with children from low socioeconomic circumstances. Each school placed specific emphasis on the importance of standards and the need for improvement, and on ways of keeping teachers and students focused on these. They also shared a strong commitment within the school communities to the belief that all students can achieve. School principals demonstrated strong leadership and recognized that leadership must extend into the classroom. They also understood that accountability, commitment and motivation grow with involvement, and sought to develop teams with a strong sense of ownership for changes made in the schools.

While studies such as these provide useful leads, too often they imply that there is a 'recipe' for improving schools in difficult circumstances, somewhere, if only we can find it. In our view this underestimates the social nature of the way practice evolves in particular schools, in particular contexts, at particular times (Wagner 1997; Robinson 1998; Wenger 1998; Ainscow et al. 2003a). The evidence presented in this book, leads us to argue that a more appropriate way forward would be to focus on determining the right sort of 'ingredients' mixed to suit the contexts and circumstances of individual schools.

We are also conscious of the danger of separating the challenge of urban school improvement from a consideration of the impact of wider social and political factors. This danger is referred to by a number of researchers who argue that there must be holistic reforms that connect schools, communities and external political and economic institutions (e.g. Anyon 1997; Crowther et al. 2003; Lipman 2004; Levin 2005). These authors conclude that it is insufficient to focus solely on the improvement of individual schools. Rather, such efforts must be part of a larger overarching plan for system-wide reform (Anyon 1997). Such a plan must include all stakeholders: at the national, district, institutional and community levels.

School reform in England

In England, recent years have seen major developments in the education system, including concentrated efforts to improve those schools that serve disadvantaged populations in urban contexts. These developments have taken the form of a series of national policy initiatives focusing on school self-management, on the quality of school leadership and teaching, the unleashing of market forces and the strengthening of accountability frameworks. Overall the evidence is that these strategies have had a positive impact on the overall performance of the system, although the debate continues as to the true extent of the progress made (e.g. Gorard 2000; Machin et al. 2005 Tymms, 2004). However, challenges remain which have, thus far, proved resistant to these strategies. These challenges centre around the performance of groups of learners whose attainment levels tend to remain low, despite vigorous institutional improvement measures and targeted interventions. Such groups include learners from certain ethnic minority communities, those from disrupted or dysfunctional family backgrounds and others whose behaviour is challenging. These groups are also a common feature of neighbourhoods that are marked by social and economic disadvantage in major cities and post-industrial towns, where low achieving learners tend to be concentrated and where the life chances of those learners remain firmly anchored to their own disadvantaged family and community backgrounds. Post-school opportunities for these learners within the immediate physical and work environments are also rather limited.

The studies that form the basis of this book thus coincide with a period of considerable educational debate in England about ways of improving the life chances of students in urban schools. This emphasis emerged largely as a result of the increasing numbers of schools defined in various ways as 'failing' in the context of the government's efforts to 'raise standards'. The resources invested have been significant, yet we still find that for many children socioeconomic status remains the best predictor of educational performance.

The development of the current English reforms can be traced back to the neo-liberal agenda of the Conservative government of the 1980s and early 1990s. In particular, the passing of the 1988 Educational Reform Act and the introduction of the National Curriculum signalled a shift in approach. This was followed in 1992 by further legislation that led to the creation of a national inspection system and the introduction of school performance 'league tables', based on student performance in a series of standardized national tests and examinations. Such measures sharply increased accountability – both inside the school and between the school and its various stakeholders. They also provided the measures that led to what Le Grand and Bartlett (1993) describe as a 'quasi-market', in which schools compete for both numbers and quality of students.

More recently, 'New Labour' governments have compounded this situation through their commitment to the principles of 'choice' and 'diversity'. On the one hand, it seems that policymakers believe competition to be an essential ingredient if the much needed 'transformation' of the education system is to be realized. On the other, the situation has become increasingly complicated by the introduction of a number of separate policy initiatives that have sought to bring about collaboration between schools (e.g. Excellence in Cities, Education Action Zones and, more recently, the Leadership Incentive Grant). This means that the current policy context is governed by a complex pattern of attempts to develop collaborative practices within an environment that remains essentially competitive. Inevitably this situation has led to a range of tensions and dilemmas for both schools and local education authorities (LEAs).

During this period of multiple government initiatives, the national inspection system has often been looked to as a source of information about those areas of school performance that needed to be tackled. It has, therefore, become a major influence on policy development. At the same time, it constitutes the government's central strategy for addressing the problem of schools at risk of failure.

Inspections are conducted by independent teams of inspectors, who make judgements against prescribed criteria about, inter alia, the quality of teaching and learning, the quality of leadership and the levels of student attainment. *The Office for Standards in Education Handbook*, sets out the criteria used in the inspection process and this is available to schools, who are therefore aware of the bases for judgement. The outcomes of inspection are published in a report, which is a public document. If a school is judged as failing (or likely to fail) to provide an acceptable standard of education, it is made subject to 'special measures' (see below). According to the Office for Standards in Education (Ofsted), a school is failing when 'there is substantial underachievement. That is, where standards are either well below the national averages for schools of that type, or consistently well below pupils' demonstrable capability, or both' (Ofsted 1993a: Part 5, p. 94, para. II).

Underachievement and low levels of attainment among students, a high proportion of unsatisfactory teaching, and ineffective leadership, are seen as the most consistent features of failing schools (Ofsted 1997: 8). However, there are many who feel that the system is more likely to identify schools in challenging circumstances as 'failing', while schools in more affluent areas are likely to be given the benefit of the doubt.

Inevitably, being placed in special measures can be a traumatic experience for all concerned, with predictable impact on the morale and self-esteem of staff and students alike. Stark (1998) has questioned whether 'naming and shaming' in this way may make it even more difficult to rebuild the confidence needed to turn a school around. In the difficult urban contexts that interest us here, relationships between school and community are often fragile, and it is not clear how the public identification of a school as 'failing' is likely to improve relationships.

The English policy framework

Ensuring that the system serves *all* students is arguably the major challenge facing the English education system, as in many other countries in the developed world. Although the government boasts of improvements in national test and examination results, many students still feel marginalized, others are excluded because of their behaviour and a significant minority are separated into special education provision. Meanwhile, school attendance is often below 90 percent in urban contexts and, following the 2005 publication of national examination results, it was widely reported that some 30,000 youngsters had just left school without any qualifications at all. This latter group included disproportionate numbers from economically deprived areas and from certain minority ethnic groups (Machin et al. 2005). At the same time, some teachers report high levels of stress and there are particular problems with teacher retention in urban contexts.

The significance of the initiatives that have been taken to address these challenges can only be understood if they are viewed within the context of the wider developments in the English education service over the last 20 years or so. In particular, there has been an intensification of political interest in education, especially regarding standards and the management and governance of the state system. This led to a variety of legislative efforts to improve schools during the 1980s, culminating in a series of acts of Parliament, of which the 1988 Education Reform Act was the most significant. These Acts were consolidated by further legislation in the early 1990s and continued by the Labour government that came into office in 1997.

Broadly speaking, there are four key elements of government policy that, taken together, have provided the context within which LEAs have been required to operate over the last few years (Ainscow et al. 2000). First of all, they are required to have *Educational Development Plans* (EDPs) in which they must describe their proposals for approval by the Secretary of State, setting out performance targets, a school improvement programme and a range of supporting information. Then, the *Code of Practice on LEA-School Relations* makes explicit the principles, expectations, powers and responsibilities that must guide the work of LEAs in relation to schools. In particular, it lays down the principle that LEA intervention in schools must be 'in inverse proportion to success', and places clear responsibility on LEAs to intervene in schools found to have serious weaknesses or those placed in special measures following an inspection. So, as the EDP prescribes what LEAs are required to do, the Code focuses on how it should be done. *Fair Funding* set out to clear the 'funding fog' surrounding education budgets by requiring resources to be allocated transparently and in line with a clear definition of the respective roles of schools and the LEA. Finally, the *Framework for the Inspection of Local Education Authorities* defined the basis of the inspection framework that, it is argued, will identify the strengths and weaknesses of each LEA inspected. Together, then, these four strands of government policy have determined what LEAs address, how they operate, how all of it is funded and how the whole process is monitored and evaluated.

Over a period of less than 20 years, therefore, the governance of the education service in England has been fundamentally changed. These changes have, perhaps, been reflected most significantly in the evolving relationships between schools, and between schools and their LEA. In particular, schools have become much less dependent on their LEAs. This movement from *dependency* towards greater *independence* has been consistently orchestrated through legislation and associated guidance from the Department for Education and Skills (DfES). This shift was summarized in the government's 1997 consultation document, 'Excellence in Schools', which stated that the 'role of LEAs is not to control schools, but to challenge all schools to improve and support those which need help to raise standards'.

The relationship between schools has also changed. Competition between schools is seen to be one of the keys to 'driving up standards' and further reducing the control of the local authority over provision. This was encouraged through the introduction of grant-maintained status for schools (now referred to as 'foundation schools') and open enrolment, supported by the publication of league tables of school results. All of this was intended to 'liberate' schools from the bureaucracy of local government and to establish a form of market place, in which effective schools would have an 'arms-length' relationship with the LEA and, indeed, with each other (Thrupp 2001). Indeed, at the time of writing, the government is actively promoting the idea of 'independent specialist schools' and has launched a programme to replace failing urban schools with so called 'academies'. These schools, which are in part privately funded, are exempt from LEA control and freed from adherence to the National Curriculum. Several such schools are funded by fundamentalist Christian sponsors and concern has been expressed about their practices of exclusion (Harris 2005).

Leadership practice

The studies we report in this book were carried out in this confusing policy context. We also contextualized them in a literature review that examined theoretical contributions, empirical studies, and accounts of educational leadership written by, or about, practitioners (West et al. 2003). For the most part, the literature we reviewed showed a movement away from prescriptive models for school leadership, and acknowledged the importance of matching leadership practice to context. For example, Leithwood et al. (1999) suggest that with the increasing diversity of schools, school leaders will need to thrive on uncertainty, have a greater capacity for collective problem solving, and become much more responsive to local needs and priorities. Fullan (2001) describes five mutually reinforcing components necessary for effective leadership in times of change: moral purpose, understanding the change process, relationship building, knowledge creation and sharing, and coherence making. Again, these are important contextualizing processes. Sergiovanni (1992) also points to the new challenges presented by student behaviour and attitudes, and argues that current approaches to school leadership may actually be getting in the way of improvement efforts. He suggests that a more responsive approach, grounded in a clear notion of the school as and within a 'community', is required.

Adopting a somewhat similar perspective, Lambert et al. (1995) argue for what they describe as a constructivist view of leadership. This is defined as 'the reciprocal processes that enable participants in an educational community to construct common meanings that lead toward a common purpose about schooling'. They use this perspective to argue that leadership involves an interactive process entered into by both students and teachers. Consequently, there is a need for shared leadership, with the principal seen as a 'leader of leaders'. Hierarchical structures have to be replaced by mechanisms that share responsibilities in a community that becomes characterized by agreed values and hopes, such that many of the control functions associated with school leadership become less important or even counter-productive. Nowhere are values and hopes more important than in our inner-city schools, where finding ways to break with history and raise expectations all round are vital to regeneration.

Much of the literature on the role of leadership in relation to school improvement places emphasis on the importance of social relationships (Hopkins et al. 1994). Johnson and Johnson (1989), two key figures in the field of social psychology, argue that leaders may structure staff working relationships in one of three ways: competitively, individualistically or cooperatively. Within a competitive structure, teachers work against each other to achieve a goal that only a few can attain; an individualistic structure exists when teachers work alone to accomplish goals that are unrelated to the goals of their colleagues; whereas a cooperative structure exists when teachers coordinate their efforts to achieve joint goals. They go on to argue that to maximize the productivity of a school, principals have to: challenge the status quo of traditional competitive and individualistic approaches to teaching; inspire a clear mutual vision of what the school should and could be; empower staff through cooperative teamwork; lead by example, using co-operative procedures and taking risks; and encouraging staff members to persist and keep striving to improve their expertise. Again, these are approaches that we have found relevant in our own studies of schools that have achieved and sustained success in urban contexts (West et al. 2005).

It is probably not mere coincidence that this rethinking of the nature of leadership practice in educational contexts is mirrored by writers who focus on business contexts. For example, Bass (1997), one of the most prolific writers on leadership topics over the past quarter of a century, argues that the dominance of transactional approaches in industrial, military and educational contexts has been challenged in the past 20 years or so by changing values and expectations in the workforce. He suggests that this has resulted in a new 'transformational' paradigm that better suits these new expectations and more accurately describes the practices of 'the best of leaders'. Denton (1998) argues that new approaches to leadership within organizations require a deliberate and conscious focus on learning, the development of a 'blame-free culture' that encourages risk-taking and experimentation and the commitment to create, transfer and use knowledge. And Senge (1990) starts from the premise that it is no longer sufficient to conceive leadership as 'figuring it out' from the top, noting that the 'organizations that will truly excel in the future will be the organizations that discover how to tap people's commitment and capacity to learn at all levels in an organization'. He goes on to argue that what will distinguish 'learning organizations' from their traditional 'controlling' counterparts will be the mastery of certain basic principles, which he describes as 'new component technologies', capable of transforming and of creating a framework for continuous improvement. Once more, we find resonance here with the descriptions of leadership practice in unusually effective schools (see, for example, Levine and Lezotte 1990).

The most helpful theoretical and empirical contexts for our work, however, are provided by Riehl (2000), who develops 'a comprehensive approach to school administration and diversity', focusing specifically on the work of school principals. As a result of a large-scale review of the relevant research literature, she concludes that school leaders need to attend to three broad types of task: fostering new meanings about diversity; promoting inclusive practices within schools; and building connections between schools and communities. She goes on to consider how these tasks can be accomplished, exploring how the concept of practice, especially discursive practice, can contribute to a fuller understanding of the work of school principals. This analysis leads the author to offer a more positive view of the potential for school principals to engage in inclusive, transformative developments. She concludes: 'When wedded to a relentless commitment to equity, voice, and social justice, administrators' efforts in the tasks of sensemaking, promoting inclusive cultures and practices in schools, and building positive relationships outside of the school may indeed foster a new form of practice' (Riehl 2000: 71). Crucially, for schools in areas of high deprivation, such leaders also ensure that teachers have the emotional and practical support needed to bring about improvements (Cotton 1991).

Levers for change

As we have explained, recent years in England have been especially interesting ones for those of us who are interested in the improvement of schools. They have provided us with opportunities to participate in and study what has probably been the most intensive attempt so far to bring about system-wide improvement. Inevitably, those areas of the system that appear to be lagging behind have received particular attention – hence the range of initiatives targeted on schools in urban contexts. The chapters that follow describe a series of studies carried out by a group of researchers from the University of Manchester on the impact of some of these initiatives.

Most of this work has involved the use of an approach to research that we refer to as 'collaborative inquiry'. This approach advocates practitioner research, carried out in partnership with academics, as a means of developing better understandings of educational processes (Ainscow 1999). Lewin's dictum that you cannot understand an organization until you try to change it is, perhaps, the clearest justification for this approach (Schein 2001). In practical terms, we believe that such understanding is best developed as a result of 'outsiders', such as ourselves, working alongside teachers, headteachers, local authority staff and other stakeholders as they attempt to move practice forward by seeking practical solutions to the complex problems posed by policy implementation. We argue that this approach can be used to overcome the traditional gap between research and practice. Some suggest that educational research *is* directly relevant to issues of practice 'if only the right people would listen'. But, what is proposed here is an alternative view, in line with the formulation made by Robinson (1998). This suggests that research findings may well continue to be ignored, regardless of how well they are communicated, if they bypass the ways in which practitioners formulate the problems they face and the constraints within which they work.

The potential benefits of collaborative inquiry, in which an open dialogue between practitioners and researchers can develop, are considerable. The ideal we aspire to is a process through which critical and self-critical reflection leads to understandings that can have an immediate and direct impact on the development of thinking and practice in the field. However, it has to be recognized that participatory research of this kind is fraught with difficulties, not least in terms of developing ways to ensure findings that both move schools on and have relevance to a wider audience.

With this in mind, we find it useful to think in terms of 'levers for change'. In his influential book, *The Fifth Discipline*, Peter Senge (1990) suggests that 'levers' are actions that can be taken that have the effect of moving practice forward by changing the behaviour of an organization and those individuals within it. He goes on to argue that those who wish to encourage change within an organization must be smart in determining where the high leverage lies. Too often, he suggests, the approaches used to bring about changes in organizations are 'low leverage'. That is to say, they may change the way things look, but not the way they work. Our aim, therefore, has been to identify what may turn out to be more subtle, less obvious and yet higher leverage strategies to bring about sustainable change in urban schools.

The arguments presented in the subsequent chapters are linked to this central concern. We believe that they are worthy of wider consideration because they are well grounded in research evidence drawn from experience in the field. At the same time, we have tried to avoid the temptation to be prescriptive, recognizing the importance of contextual factors and how they bear on the way schools operate. Accordingly, we present many examples (not exemplars), since our main purpose is to assist readers in relating the ideas that are presented to their own contexts.

The chapters are loosely grouped in relation to developing themes. Following this introductory chapter, Chapters 2 to 5 look closely at the experience of those involved in urban schools that face challenging circumstances. In Chapters 2 and 3, Nicolaidou and Ainscow, and Morley focus on developments in urban primary schools that have been designated as failing following an inspection. A feature of both of these chapters is that the authors get close to the action in ways that are unusual in such sensitive contexts. Similarly, in Chapter 4, Ainscow and Howes present a detailed account of their frustrated efforts to foster developments in practice with staff partners in an urban secondary school that is going through a period of considerable turbulence. Staying in the secondary sector, in Chapter 5, West, Ainscow and Stanford report on their analysis of developments in a group of urban secondary schools where sustainable progress appears to have occurred. In this chapter, as with the earlier ones, there is a strong emphasis on listening to the voice of practitioners. This helps us to make sense of the realities they face. It also illustrates the way that well intended national reform efforts can create barriers to progress.

The next group of chapters focuses on various attempts to move practice forward in the field. Together these chapters illustrate what we see as untapped resources that exist within the system. In Chapter 6, Helen Gunter describes the experience of a group of city schools that worked together to address difficulties. Chapter 7 moves to the level of the school district. Here Ainscow, Howes and Tweddle analyse their research in an English LEA that has a strong reputation for urban school improvement. This leads them to conclude that much of this success involves the orchestration of expertise that lies within that authority through processes of collaboration. This theme continues in Chapter 8, where Ainscow, West and Nicolaidou describe the way three successful secondary schools worked with a school that was in difficulties to bring about improvements in its policies and practices. Noting that the impact was apparent in all four of the schools, they see this experience as pointing towards a new paradigm for school improvement, one that requires groups of schools to collaborate.

The idea of school to school collaboration is picked up and further analysed in the subsequent two chapters. In Chapter 9, Fox and Ainscow describe their experience of working with a 'think-tank' of headteachers to develop forms of leadership that encourage mutual learning. While the outcomes of their work are very promising, they are left uncertain as to whether it is possible to extend the use of such approaches because of what they see as the perverse requirements of national strategies. More encouraging in this respect is the study reported by Howes and Ainscow in Chapter 10, which illustrates how all the secondary schools in one city worked together to address the challenge of underachievement among students. In Chapter 11 Alan Dyson cautions against making assumptions about the extent to which schools can make a difference and puts the case for locating school improvement efforts within a broader strategy for urban regeneration. This leads him to raise important questions about current theories of school leadership. Finally, in Chapter 12, we reflect on the findings of all of this research in order to draw out the implications for the development of policy and practice in the field.

2

THE EXPERIENCE OF FAILURE IN URBAN PRIMARY SCHOOLS

Maria Nicolaidou and Mel Ainscow

As we noted in Chapter 1, inspection has been a central strategy in the English approach to improving achievement in urban schools. Where schools are seen to 'fail' an inspection this is intended to focus efforts on rapid improvement strategies. This chapter looks closely at the experience of schools that have experienced such an approach. The study is unusual in that researchers have often found it difficult to gain access to such sensitive contexts. The detailed analysis of what happened in the schools suggests that the experience of being characterized as 'failing' can act as a barrier to the creation of more colla- borative ways of working. This analysis leads to an examination of the links between culture and leadership, and how such links can provide useful insights for school improvement in contexts that are defined as failing.

With the introduction of the national inspection system in the early 1990s, a number of schools were judged unable to provide an acceptable standard of education. This focused attention on the nature of their problems. There is little research available that looks closely at what happens in these schools, not least because gaining access to such sensitive contexts is usually difficult, if not impossible.

In this chapter we report on the findings of a study conducted in English primary schools placed in 'special measures' following an inspection. All the schools served economically poor inner city districts. The schools were each visited on a daily basis for about seven weeks in order to observe classroom teaching, to interview headteachers, teaching and non-teaching staff, and LEA officers, and to examine archive material and documents. In what follows we provide a flavour of life in the schools. This leads us to focus on barriers to progress and the implications for improvement efforts.

Improvement through inspection?

In England, the government's notion of providing support for schools at risk of failure has been mainly through the national system of inspection. 'Improvement through inspection' was the slogan used when this strategy was introduced.

Underachievement and poor performance, high levels of unsatisfactory teaching, and ineffective or total lack of leadership are the factors that Ofsted considers as the most consistent features of failing schools (Ofsted 1997: 8). However, schools tend to present a combination of the above factors, and as others argue, 'it is the degree, combination and cumulation of these characteristics that causes the judgement that a school is failing' (Myers 1995: 8). It is therefore imperative to understand that based on these circumstances there can be no single solution that can best serve schools in 'special measures'. In other words, there can be no widely used recipe for improving schools in such challenging circumstances.

Being considered to be a failing school, and hence placed in special measures, is a traumatic experience for those directly involved. Teachers report on how their professionalism and self-belief is damaged. It is widely argued that by attributing responsibilities publicly and stigmatizing a school as having failed its pupils, its internal capacities to change may be disabled (Stark 1998; Stoll and Myers 1998, 2003; Nicolaidou 2002).

Through our research we were able to experience something of what it is like to be a teacher in a school in special measures. This led to a series of extended case studies (Nicolaidou 2005). Here, we can only present a summary of these accounts. Nevertheless, these summaries offer at least a flavour of their experiences.

What follows, then, is a short 'guided tour' of three of the schools, focusing specifically on the behaviour and actions of their headteachers, using the voices of some of those involved in order to give a sense of what occurred.

Parkside

Inadequate leadership and management was one of the issues identified during the inspection of Parkside primary school. More specifically, it was judged that there was no clear vision as to how improvement might be achieved. The inspectors also commented that the headteacher did not delegate power to key members of her staff.

Some staff argued that their headteacher seemed to be lacking several characteristics of the kind the leader needed in order to turn around a failing school. For example, one commented:

> I don't think she's got strong management skills, or a strong sense of direction. I don't think she knows what she is doing or where we are going. She is not experienced enough for the post she has and I don't think she knows what's happening. She is not experienced enough to

deal with these issues adequately. She stays in her office, so kids know that they'll get away with things. She is just not strong enough.

(Teacher)

Another teacher saw the problem as being one of limited experience:

The teachers feel that it would have been better if the head had worked in other schools and had the experience of different approaches and styles. She became a head at a very early age ... she is kind with the children and the staff but she is most of the times in her office; she is not managing by walking about in a sense. I don't think she knows what she is doing or where we are going

(Teacher)

Another commented on the head's apparent insensitivity to the concerns of her staff:

She sometimes neglects to hear the staff and the signals we send out to her. For example, the planning was too much and we all moaned about it. When we strongly said 'Planning: no more', she turned round and said 'Oh dear is it starting to bother you?'

(Teacher)

In some instances, such concerns were extended beyond the head to include the way her senior team was working:

There are too many initiatives in the school being done because they [the senior team] were told to and not because they themselves identified that was needed. Most of the time the pupils miss out on other areas of the curriculum and get tired by it. For example, they were told that we needed to improve the handwriting in school so we started doing handwriting for half an hour ever day after lunch. The pupils got bored with it, and then they realised that this was being done on the expense of the silent reading that they stopped doing since ... there is a lack of general overview of the situation from the top, meaning the head and the SMT. They are missing the broader picture of the situation. They should be able to see that. I think there is a communication problem in school from the top to the staff and the other way round.

(Teacher)

Some members of staff felt that the headteacher was overly defensive. A few added that, although she did ask their opinion at times, she did not always listen to them. As a result, there was a general impression that she wanted to do everything her way:

She [the headteacher] does not like challenges. The only way she can cope is by doing it her way and not getting into confrontations, because she may not handle that. She is very friendly with the staff and does not wish for the staff to be against her. She would feel very upset if we did. She takes things personally.

(Teacher)

For her part, the headteacher felt unsupported by the LEA, both when she was first appointed and in the period following the inspection. Some members of staff also indicated that the LEA had not provided the support she had needed as a young headteacher. On the other hand, LEA officers felt that the head had not disclosed to them the extent of the problems in the school:

> I think [the headteacher] has deliberately ignored our advice at times. So much so, that the action plan was rejected the first time. She was told, in no uncertain terms that she had to listen to the LEA the second time round. She followed our rules fine, but it was almost a question of 'you don't need to tell me'. I think she has seen the whole thing as a personal 'slur' on her. I guess she knows that we are still watching. It's a difficult one really. On the surface, she smiles and she's pleasant and she's quite sweet. But, underneath there is a resistance.
>
> (LEA officer)

The account of Parkside illustrates the way inspection can lead to a collapse of confidence in leaders within a school community, and between the school and the LEA staff whose role it is to provide support. As a result, an atmosphere of blame permeates the context in a way that undermines efforts to bring staff together around a common purpose. The account indicates the need for intensive support for those who take on leading roles in failing schools.

St Pauls

Described to us as the worst school in the LEA, our first impression was one of neglect, especially the school building which was in urgent need of attention. St Pauls serves a well established ethnic minority community not far from the city centre. Both school and staff appeared to have been caught in a time warp. Most of the teachers had been at the school for 15 to 20 years and seemed to have got on with their work with little reference to the changes that had occurred during that period.

Once again, this was a school that was said to have a history of inefficient leadership and management. The previous headteacher, although he was characterized by teachers as a nice person, had, we were told, rarely managed to bring about any significant changes in policy and practice. Some staff described their frustrations with what had happened. At the same time, there had remained a sense of complacency, referred to by one teacher as a culture of 'it will do'.

Following the inspection the head retired and the LEA encouraged the governors to appoint a successor with a successful record of working in failing schools. This was seen as a significant step in breaking down existing attitudes:

> [The staff] were in complete denial of [their situation]. So, they needed somebody who didn't go along with 'but we've always done it like this'.

That's what the school needed, a complete break; and at that instance a total and complete break from the past.

(LEA officer)

Some staff reacted positively, seeing the new headteacher as being the answer to all their prayers. One commented, 'She gets things done and she is fair as well'. There was general agreement, too, that she was 'very professional' and familiar with what needed to be done to move the school forward. This provided them with some sense of security.

However, her actions were not always received favourably:

When you are doing what I am doing you should not expect to make friends, but enemies, because people don't like to hear the truth ... I won't take sides but staff in crisis always want you to take their side ... Yes I do [intimidate the staff]. I know I do. Now, it is because usually they are a lazy lot and somebody has to 'crack the whip'. Even if 'crack the whip' says 'look if you don't get your finger out, we're going to close this school, and I can always find a job in schools that have problems, can you find another job?' ... It is pointless not to involve the staff because if at the end this school stays open, I won't be here. They have to learn to stand on their own feet

(Headteacher)

One of the head's aims was to encourage staff to become a self-supporting team. She was also keen that they should have ownership of the development of their school. However, initially some staff disputed the motives behind some of her actions. At the same time, she perhaps failed to realize how demoralized many of the staff were. Thus, during her first few months in the school she applied more pressure on the staff than they were ready to accept:

I think in some respects it was my mistake last term, because they were in denial and I was often seen to be on the wrong side, in their opinion. I won't take sides but staff in crisis always want you to take their side ... they could not handle it. I realised that what I did last term was to put too much pressure on them. Now they receive one target per week. Previously I had given them a long list of the things needed to see through and they did not need that; now I've broken this list up, but for some this is still too much.

(Headteacher)

Gradually the headteacher delegated more power to the staff. For example, the structure of staff meetings gradually changed. Now, there was a written agenda, and a member of staff was responsible for chairing the meeting and making a presentation about one of the themes for discussion. In this way, staff confidence grew, such that there was a greater sense of trust in the head and the changes she was encouraging.

St Pauls was eventually taken out of special measures. It seemed that in this particular context, the appointment of an outsider who had previous experience in working with schools facing difficulties provided a sense of confidence and common purpose in a school that had previously lost its way.

However, there remained questions about the sustainability of the improvements that occurred, particularly if the headteacher were to leave.

Grange

A new headteacher was appointed to Grange primary school just prior to an inspection. The school was already in special measures and had had an acting headteacher, the deputy head, for a period of 12 months. A few months after the inspection, leadership and management were judged to be 'very good'. Indeed, the report commented that the new headteacher had been successful in gaining the respect and support of the governing body, the parents, the local education authority and the pupils.

The new headteacher seemed to have had a clear plan for taking the school forward and consciously tried to share this vision with his staff members. It was noticeable that he frequently used catch phrases, such as 'everyone an achiever', to boost people's confidence. In this way, he appeared to demonstrate his own high expectations for the school and this seemed to be picked up by those around him.

During one conversation, the headteacher mused that he would like the school to achieve Beacon status in order that it could become 'a vehicle for social change in the area'. He added:

> I want us to be in a situation where as a vibrant, successful part of this community we are actually beginning to have an influence and an impact beyond the narrow education issues.

However, some staff were less convinced. They argued that the head was very directive and authoritarian, noting that he 'was not prepared to meet people half way'. Many felt that, despite what he said, decision-making lay mostly with him. Some added that his tendency to share power with a few members of staff may have increased the sense of insecurity felt by the majority.

On the other hand, the headteacher, while noting such comments, stressed that his aim was to create a new ethos so that the Grange would be 'working as a school'. In order to do that, he would need to have staff willing to follow and be led, but also to lead as well. He summed this up as follows:

> I'm not by nature directive, I don't want to have my finger on every single pulse, once I have staff I have confidence in. The reality of special measures is that one has to move in very quickly and make arrangements to meet the needs of the school.

Therefore, since he was clear that his priority was to change what he saw as the dominant culture, the children's needs would come first. Explaining the possible implications of this, he commented, that he could not 'get the job done and have the teachers pleased too'. Over the next few months managing the tensions that arose due to different interests within the staffroom proved difficult, especially when some teachers saw their powers removed and vested in newly appointed members of staff.

Like the earlier two accounts, the story of Grange illustrates the way different perceptions and interests shape what happens as stakeholders respond to the sense of pressure that is associated with the experience of special measures. In such contexts headteachers are faced with many strategic dilemmas, not least those that arise as a result of the tension between the need to focus efforts on externally determined goals and the desire to foster involvement of staff in improvement efforts.

Leadership

Although this study did not begin as a study of leadership, it emerged as a significant theme. Indeed, the study reinforced the argument that places leadership at the heart of organizational culture and change. The study also enhanced our understanding of the peculiarities school leaders are faced with in schools in 'special measures'.

The emergent theme of leadership reminded us of Bales's (1952, 1953) theory of group systems. As with leaderless groups, the headteachers were called on to solve problems of communication and organization that the group members were faced with in relation to the task of turning their schools round. The existence of such problems added to the tension between establishing cohesion and achieving the task in the way that Bales suggests. This points to the need for leaders who can foster both task- and people-centred behaviours among their colleagues.

Although much has been said about which style of leadership best facilitates organizational change, we are left feeling that no one particular form of leadership style can work in schools in special measures. In such contexts headteachers have to be 'flexible' and adopt a variety of leadership styles and strategies at different moments, in other words be directive, facilitative, transformational and/or transactional, in order to bring about cultural change and improvement (see also Harris and Chapman 2002). Their behaviour has to be influenced by what they are trying to achieve and how well their propositions will be accepted by their followers (in this case, the staff and pupils). Our data illustrates that leadership is both influenced by and impacts on its followers' subcultures. In the school accounts, the headteachers' behaviour seemed related to staff willingness to adopt change. Indeed, the study indicated that unless staff were willing to accept suggestions for improvement, there was little that the headteachers could do.

The evidence from this study underlines the importance of organizational culture in fostering improvement and development. This leads us to conclude that it is through the careful study of local practices in relation to their contexts that we can proceed to making suggestions for future development (Ainscow 1998).

Understanding practices in relation to cultures (how people think and interact) we can learn to appreciate how peoples' own interests may become an obstacle to development. What the case studies suggest is that the schools, and in particular the schools' leaders, needed to take into consideration such matters when trying to establish their 'new' ways of working. This would then facilitate 'participation' and, in this way, people would be motivated in making changes for themselves. If staff realize that the improvement process is 'less ego-endangering' for their workplace, then 'the more they will request and offer advice and assistance to accomplish agreed-upon goals' (Rosenholtz 1989: 6). As Hargreaves and Hopkins (1991) argue, it is only when teachers recognize a personal and professional gain from a task that they will be motivated and committed to it. Consequently, any strategy used needs to be one that will bridge all arguments and unite the staff around a common purpose, that of improvement and development.

The need to achieve unity and harmony between staff was significant for each of these schools. Because of the intensity of the situations they faced, the 'special measures' period was one full of tension, conflicts and clashes of personal agendas – especially regarding professional development. In this sense, special measures presented barriers to staff collaboration. The findings suggest that staff needed to be brought together in ways that would foster more positive working relationships among colleagues – the pathway towards becoming a 'moving' school (Rosenholtz 1989).

The shaping of such a workplace culture has to be realized in the light of existing beliefs and shared history that hold all the pieces of the jigsaw together. In establishing a new set of beliefs and values, the aim should be for the staff to become the co-founders and, simultaneously, bearers of a new culture (Nias et al. 1989). One important feature of this 'new' culture would be positive staff relationships. As demonstrated in our accounts, staff relationships were fragmented and at times led to serious confrontations. Positive relationships needed to be manifested in the form of a collaborative culture (Hargreaves 1994). Staff had to be encouraged to work in collaboration, share practices and engage in teamwork and co-planning.

The task of creating a 'new' culture leads to what Hargreaves and Hopkins (1991) refer to as the 'maintenance/development dilemma'; in other words, the need to maintain some continuity between the schools' past, present and future. They argue that schools need to achieve such a continuity, 'partly to provide the stability which is the foundations of new developments and partly because the reforms do not by any means change everything that schools now do' (1991: 17). Our accounts illustrate that such a tension is always a possibility. For example, it was observed that future developments were at times endangered by what Reynolds (1991) refers to as 'cling-ons' to past practices.

The 'maintenance/development dilemma' also has implications for the micropolitics of the school. This relates to the ideas of Bales, referred to earlier, and points to the possible friction arising around issues of power. Bales, and Hargreaves and Hopkins, signify that in such situations those in the leadership structures of a school have a vital role to play – especially the headteacher, who has to help those in school to 'develop an agreed perspective on how the tension' can be resolved (Reynolds 1991: 21) so that both pressures are balanced. Such efforts, Hargreaves and Hopkins note, are likely to involve cultural change; the way the tension is balanced will then become an expression of the school's culture (Reynolds 1991: 17). However, the efforts to address the maintenance/development dilemma, are not likely to be successful 'if the existing management arrangements are assumed to be adequate for supporting development simply because they have worked well in the past in ensuring maintenance' (Reynolds 1991: 18). Thus, adjustments to the management and leadership arrangements of the school are more than likely to be needed.

Moving practice forward

We argue, therefore, that in schools facing challenges, leadership is an important lever that can help to facilitate improvement efforts. The head-teachers in this study were often faced with unpredictability and conflict, and their interpersonal skills were often called on. This suggests that one of the 'requirements' of headteachers in such schools is to be people-centred and provide moral support to the members of the school community. In this sense, headteachers have to provide for and ensure a notion of 'social capital' (Hargreaves 2003a), through the development of others.

On this analysis, we are led to conclude that leadership has to involve the use of different approaches in schools that are considered to be failing. So, for example, during the initial stages where the situation is likely to be both irrational and emotionally charged, the headteacher probably needs to adopt a more directive and prescriptive leadership style in order to facilitate the establishment of systems, structures and procedures; in other words, there is a need to be more task-oriented. Ideally this should lead to a stage where the school's internal capacities for renewal will steadily begin to be restored to health. Then, the leader should be able to adopt a more empowering and democratic leadership approach in order to inspire others, and create a common set of values and norms that will increase staff commitment. This will once again take the school and the staff to another stage where, hopefully out of special measures, a more dispersed leadership style can be adopted (Spillane et al. 2001).

The idea, then, is to move from a tight to a more loosely coupled system (Weick 1976) in order to encourage responsiveness and flexibility. Tight coupling will be needed in terms of systems and procedures. In this way the schools will be more able to survive, meet the external demands and internally integrate these new systems to adopt a new culture that facilitates improvement. This is reinforced by Hopkins (2000), who argues that in times of instability and change, 'there is a need to tighten the loose coupling, to increase collaboration and to establish more fluid and responsive structures' (2000: 8).

It is important here to note that two of the headteachers of the schools in this study were brought in either just before the schools went into special measures or soon after in order to 'turn them round'; such an approach bears resemblance to the 'super-heads' of the Fresh Start initiative. However, the headteachers were seen to be struggling to achieve their tasks, and even HMI found them to be isolated and signalled that there have to be ways of sup-porting these headteachers. The headteachers were linked with other heads or educational consultants. They explained how productive this had been for them and their schools. However, they argued that such initiatives should have been better facilitated. Our experience of other projects (see in particular Chapter 8, in this book), reinforces the case for leadership support networks. However, this approach raises some questions about the sustainability of the improvement efforts once such support is withdrawn.

In the same way, the issue of sustainability is also raised for two of the headteachers in this study whose engagement with the school would most probably end once the schools were out of 'special measures'. The other school presented a different problem: its headteacher took the school into special measures. This brought a number of different challenges and, in a way, strengthened the resistance the school exhibited to external support, since the headteacher was observed to be defensive of her school and, at times, towards her staff. This was seen to have an impact on the improvement efforts.

The educational reform agenda in England and Wales has, in recent years, introduced increased autonomy for schools, since it was felt that the 'over-protectiveness' of LEAs had led to a sense of dependence that hindered the required improvement in educational quality. However, Ainscow et al. (2002) argue that an approach that relies solely on individual schools developing their own improvement strategies is, similarly, not able to bring about widespread progress, particularly in the context of economically poor urban contexts. It seems, then, that we may be witnessing the emergence of a 'third way', that of school to school interdependence. Indeed, as argued in later chapters, this points towards a possible new direction for school improvement policy and practice more generally. Much more is expected of schools, and such initiatives are not exactly catered for by the current national policy context. We would suggest, therefore, that further thought should be given as to how policies can be developed in order to provide greater incentives.

Most importantly, the roles of local authorities need to be revisited since their powers have been reduced within the current reform agenda in England. The evidence from our study shows that in order for the schools to focus their efforts on the pressing objective of raising standards and having special measures removed, there was a strong reliance on the LEA to provide a wide range of support at a management level as well as at a teaching level. The schools welcomed LEA support; none of them said that they could proceed with substantial improvements without the help and guidance of the LEA. Nevertheless, some within the schools felt that the LEA's lack of action had contributed to their problem. Do local authorities, therefore, have the credibility to take on the tasks necessary in order to help the schools? Acknowledging that 'the role of LEAs is not to control schools, but to challenge all schools to improve and support those which need help to raise standards' (DfEE 1997: 67), how then can an LEA know that there are problems unless it is closely involved with its schools?

Of course, it is important to recognize that the balance between prevention of problems and intervention after problems occur is a difficult one to strike. However, there does seem to be evidence of a reaction from officers in some English LEAs against the perceived pressure to stay out of schools unless they are known to be failing. For example, as part of its preparations for a recent visit from Ofsted, another LEA noted: 'This LEA, whilst recognising the parameters of the new relationship between schools and LEAs, set out by the DfEE ... must also fulfil its wider role of securing improvement in all its schools ... Prevention is better, and less expensive, than intervention' (Nicolaidou et al. 2001).

Some final thoughts

In this chapter we have reported some of the outcomes of a study carried out in a city authority in England. The schools we visited were faced with extremely difficult situations since external inspection had characterized them as failing and added that they required 'special measures' in order to be restored to health. Increased levels of stress, anxiety and insecurity accompanied this categorization.

We were fortunate to experience part of the lives of these schools. The sensitive situations we encountered confirmed our original decision to approach this study within a naturalistic, qualitative research paradigm. The particular methodological approach provided us with access to the schools' lives and helped us to become accepted by the school community to such a degree that we were able to reveal some of those taken for granted assumptions that constructed the schools' every day reality, while being considerate of the uniqueness, unpredictability and emotional strain of each situation.

Our reporting has provided us with vivid accounts of the situations these schools face, which were not available to a broader audience, since entry to such schools is usually restricted by the intensity and sensitivity of 'special measures'. Our inside observations of these very sensitive situations allow us to say that where improvement efforts have failed it is because of the idea that such schools are faced with predictable and straight forward problems. On the contrary, our understandings of such schools indicates that they are faced with complex and, simultaneously, unique issues. However, we are left feeling that such situations are very much dependent on the nature of their leadership.

We have argued that no one leadership style fits best with the peculiarities of such schools. However we need to stress the need for reflexive leadership styles that are adaptable to the schools' specific cultures. By analysing cultural assumptions in schools in special measures many insights can be derived into the way they function that can facilitate improvement efforts.

3

THE DEVELOPMENT OF LEADERSHIP CAPACITY IN A SCHOOL FACING CHALLENGING CIRCUMSTANCES

Andrew Morley

As we saw in the previous chapter, headteachers in schools facing challenging circumstances experience a series of strategic dilemmas. In particular, the need to bring about immediate improvements in order to satisfy the demands of external regulatory agencies can act as a barrier to longer term growth. This chapter uses extracts from a diary kept by the newly appointed headteacher of an inner city primary school that had been placed in special measures in order to throw further light on these issues. It shows how he and his colleagues felt about the imposition of strategies on a staff that had lost confidence in themselves. The chapter argues that the danger with such an approach is that it can lead to short-term fixes at the expense of more sustainable improvement. This leads the author to conclude that steps towards more sustainable improvement should start with the common sense understandings of the teachers involved.

In its attempts to raise standards in education in England, the government has increasingly relied on a system of school inspection. A key driver behind this approach was the demand to root out and hold to account schools that failed to provide satisfactory standards of education. As a headteacher working in such 'failing' schools, I became increasingly aware that, in its desire to achieve improvements, the government was also creating barriers to longer term, sustainable progress.

In looking for more sustainable pathways I am drawn to the argument of Willard Waller who argued, many years ago, that:

> The common sense understanding which teachers have of their problems bites deeper than the maunderings of most theorists. Teachers will do well to insist that any programme of educational reform shall start with them, that it shall be based on, and include, their common-sense insights

(Waller 1932: 457)

Bearing this in mind, in this chapter I reflect on my experience as headteacher of an inner-city primary school during a period of special measures. Using extracts from my diary and conversations with colleagues, I provide examples of 'common sense understanding and insights' and their implications for the development of sustainable school improvement.

Background of the school

Green Hill Primary School was formed as a result of the amalgamation of an infant school and a junior school in 2002. Both of the existing schools had been in special measures, the infant school for three and a half years and the junior school for one year. At the time of my appointment, I was the sixth headteacher in two years.

The school serves an economically deprived population, with 78 percent of children entitled to free school meals. The school featured in a national publication listing the 25 worst performing primary schools in the country. At the outset, relationships at the school were poor, with a number of staff and parents being in serious dispute with the governing body. As a result of a monitoring visit just prior to me taking over as headteacher, HMI noted that, 'even in terms of special measures, standards at the school were appalling'.

My initial impression was that of a school that seemed unhealthy and vulnerable. Staff felt attacked from all sides and, of course, now they had the added insecurity of a new headteacher whom they did not know. Understandably, such feelings led some members of staff to be reluctant to participate in any proposals for improvement. This was even apparent during my introductory visit to the school, when a significant number of the staff refused to meet with me.

In describing Green Hill in this way, I am conscious of adopting what might be seen as a deficit perspective, focusing only on weaknesses. In fact, such a description provides little indication of what emerged, which demonstrated the potential of the same people in bringing about improvements. Indeed, the staff who remained, plus the new recruits who joined us, proved determined in their efforts to do what was required and two years later the school was removed from special measures.

During that two year period, audit and accountability became the ruling principle that guided everything we did. The staff were acutely aware that their conduct and performance were under constant scrutiny by inspectors. Having been deemed to be failing, we were assigned an inspector from HMI, who worked with us during the period of special measures. She monitored the school, visiting every term until she was of the opinion that we were providing an acceptable standard of education.

Understanding the inspection agenda

Beverley was a teacher attached to the LEA's school improvement team. She was placed in the school as part of the LEA's plan to support and develop improvements in teaching and learning. Commenting on her role she explained:

> There is a lot of blame and the idea of support from the outside is limited. Anyone who has not worked within such schools, at a particular time, in a particular context cannot understand the problems. I do not have the answers and there is no one out there with the answers. The agenda facing these schools is externally driven by people who are in positions of power, but how can they understand the nature of the difficulties that the staff and the children face.

Her comments seem to imply a difficulty, in that the power to affect the direction of the school is externally held but, paradoxically, is limited in its capacity to impact on improvement. There seems to be a problem in the capacity of a 'snapshot' visit to understand what is needed.

In my view, any guidance provided by inspection should be produced with the intention of contributing to the knowledge of the staff, recognizing that they have a privileged understanding of the context within which they work. That is not to suggest that 'insiders' have some elite knowledge to which no one else has access. Rather, what I am saying is that those who work in a situation are aware of contextual factors and details that someone on the outside can only have a feeling for and can never fully appreciate. I suggest that practitioners have a detailed understanding of their context and should, therefore, lead in creating the direction for the school. However, in suggesting this I do so tentatively in that constant inspection can reduce the confidence of staff to take such a lead.

Tension

All inspections create a degree of tension within a school. However, when you have been in special measures for over three years this tension can cause very competent and confident teachers to react in very untypical and at times irrational ways. Take, for example, the following extract from my diary:

> I arrive at school at about 7.30 and walk around encouraging everyone, reminding them of learning objectives, pace and a happy smiley face. At about 8.30 I chat with Kate (senior teacher) who is very distressed. Apparently the previous week there were 12 mats and now there are only 11 mats for her PE lesson. I try to rationalise with her about the situation. We discuss what she could do but she starts to blame others and it seems pointless to carry on the conversation. Ten minutes later I return to her classroom but she has not calmed down and simply asks me to leave her alone ... The HMI visit Kate's PE lesson and I am worried. Thankfully the lesson went well and she has transformed from the nervous wreck to a very happy and contented person. My anger earlier in the day is lost. I am just delighted to hear positive news, pleased for her and the school.
> (4 June)

The inspection process can be very debilitating. Kate is a good teacher, with the capacity to make a significant contribution to the leadership of the school, but the pressure described above caused her to behave uncharacter-istically and taking on a leadership role would need to wait.

Another diary extract refers to Eileen, a highly skilled teacher who had a very difficult time:

> She is very worried about the inspection, not feeling confident with a lot to lose. The next day she is teaching year 6 and they can be difficult. At one point she was not going to come in, on the pretext of attending a conference. She is a very loyal person and I always believed she would not let us down, but I am worried . . . I ring her and offer to teach certain lessons. We can't afford for Eileen to fail lessons, it would be devastating for her and the school . . . On the phone she insists she wants to teach the lesson and I leave it.
>
> (12 October)

Inspection had caused Eileen, a teacher with years of successful teaching behind her, to lose confidence. As with Kate, she has real potential to con-tribute to the leadership of the school, but the competence agenda creates doubts and threatens her self-belief. When teachers feel threatened as to whether they are personally succeeding, they are less likely to contribute to getting the organization right. Both were effective teachers, with the capacity to take on leadership roles, but the tension disempowered them to the point that their involvement in leadership would be a slow process requiring sig-nificant support.

Criticism

The capacity for inspection to undermine effective teachers is furthered by the criticism that teachers in special measures are likely to face. Whether justified or not, this can be difficult to accept. Beverley, for one, found this very difficult to appreciate and she was shocked at the manner in which the 'supposed' failings of some teachers were voiced by the HMI:

> If you think of Julie and all those who were here from the start you have to ask, what is in it for them? They come at half past seven every morning and work hard, but if it goes wrong they get blamed and per-haps people are leaving because of the history of hurt, because they are hurt; and if it is true what the HMI said then it is totally repugnant . . . there is all that hurt.
>
> (Beverley)

What the HMI actually said was, 'even in terms of special measures the per-formance of the staff was appalling'. Whether this was true or not is de-batable, but what is clear is that it leaves staff feeling insecure and challenges their loyalty to the school.

Being criticized was one thing, but being placed in a subservient position to higher authority was difficult to accept:

> I do not like being watched and judged by someone I cannot have any interaction with. When Teresa and I received feedback I found it quite

offensive, that the HMIs should speak to me, someone who has been doing the job for twenty years, the way they did. It was as though I did not know anything and they simply spoke at me. I thought I was going into the room for a dialogue but they just lectured us – they spoke at us. Their job is different to ours but it does not mean they know more than us. They have insights to offer but so do we

(Beverley)

Beverley clearly sensed a hierarchy in her relationship with the school inspectors. She seemed to feel that what she had to say was irrelevant, she was merely there to listen and respond accordingly, whether she agreed or not. Sometimes this came in the form of a directive, as described above, or by being coerced into taking certain approaches as a means to prove our competence.

Shared values

The sense of subservience and lack of a voice was highlighted by the fact that the shared values necessary for the improvement of a school were largely taken out of the control of our community. When you are in special measures, what the community values does not seem to count. In practice, what counted was our ability to value and be accountable to meeting the improvement agenda, as defined by the HMI. Take, for example, the following diary extract.

We discussed at length the management structure for the school, with Key Stage Leaders and a Standards Leader being seen to be key appointments. There was lengthy discussion on the roles of these people and how it would help in the leadership of the school

(7th November)

On reflection, the structure proved to be hierarchical and totally against the more distributed and collaborative approach that I, as headteacher, preferred. There seemed to be a prescription of how the leadership should be organized, with no consideration of a different approach. Once out of special measures, this hierarchical leadership system proved to be a barrier to further progress, and significant time was spent in establishing a more participatory approach necessary to build the capacity to sustain our future.

Similarly, at each monitoring inspection there were expectations of what should be happening in the school. Following a conversation with Stephen, one of the teachers, I reflected in my diary:

He says I seem to change a lot when it comes to inspection. I suppose I am conscious of the progress needed to prove our competence, certain things needed to be done and I would create a list, with little or no consultation. I suppose I am saying to staff trust me, if we complete some simple tasks then it will get us points with the HMI.

(May)

My experience had provided an understanding of what HMI value and expect. Whether we believed this activity to make a difference was not the point – the trick was to placate the inspectors. In meeting HMI criteria our values and ownership were not the priority. This was not necessarily how I would like to work and was against the principles of my leadership vision for the school: being prescriptive, without collaboration and staff ownership. It was, however, necessary to be seen to be competent.

Thinking about teaching

At the root of our improvement strategy was a rigid 'competence-based approach' to teaching that all staff adhered to and implemented in a very prescriptive fashion. While we were not actually forced into teaching in the way we did, the strategy we employed was very much influenced by the need to fulfil certain criteria and demonstrate our competence. We knew that our practices would be measured against the criteria prescribed by Ofsted and, whether we subscribed to or valued the model we adopted did not seem to count. The type of approach I have in mind here is spelt out in an Ofsted publication *Lessons Learned from Special Measures*, which provides guidance on what constitutes effective practice.

> Learning is most effective when the learning objectives are simple, pre-cise and couched in terms which people can understand. Those teachers who share the objectives with pupils by displaying and referring to them at the beginning, middle and end of the lesson find that they keep the lesson on schedule ... and that pupils learn readily and improve their standard of work.
>
> (Ofsted 1999: 30)

Stephen, in his second year of teaching, indicated his awareness of all of this, when he said:

> You start off by writing the learning objective on the board. I always get two or three children to read it and I always come back to it. Once we understand what we are doing we do our activity and complete the lesson with the plenary ... it's about clear progression ... its formal and we keep within the boundaries. The structure ensures the children are on task and focused. You have got these little building blocks and it makes it bite sized chunks for the children.

What Stephen describes was typical practice for all of the teachers within the school. It was limited but it ensured we at least achieved a competent stan-dard, or so we thought. Stephen later reflected on a similar lesson during an HMI monitoring visit which didn't go to plan.

> I thought I'd predicted everything that was going to happen and then X, Y and Z came along that I wasn't ready for, it threw things into turmoil. I spent so long planning the lesson that I could visualize every second. This is what we are going to do, then we'll do this, but suddenly

somebody starts pulling away all these little blocks. Then it's, hang on a minute, this isn't going right and you try to put these bits in and they don't seem to fit anymore and things fall apart. I had this picture of the lesson and can see how it's going to happen, but then a child interacts in a different way and the emphasis shifts away from what you think should fit your structure. Then its problems.

In talking about this Stephen began to see the prescribed structure as a hindrance:

I was too focused on the prescription, but when it is not working you have to adapt ... you've got to be flexible. You need to refer to the objective and so on, but then somewhere in the middle you've got to do what a good teacher does and that's kind of juggle things around. This isn't working; I need to try something else.

Stephen felt he was in a straitjacket and did not have the confidence to respond. He clearly highlighted the danger of being too dependent, inflexible and lacking the confidence to use his own professional judgement. As he states, he did not have the capacity to 'juggle things around and redirect learning'. This was a new language, which didn't fit the competence agenda, and Stephen became very aware that he was being controlled and there was frustration. For example:

I don't think you need people telling you to teach like this and what you have to teach all the time. Common sense will tell you what the children will need and I think it should be down to the individual teacher to give the children the right experience

What this extract highlights is that it was only in failure that Stephen emerged from the imposed technical perspective in order to analyse his practice. In so doing, he revealed a capacity to reflect, and reflecting provided deeper insight and knowledge that proved invaluable in directing and leading the development of his teaching. By ignoring such reflections, we marginalized and rejected fundamental skills and knowledge necessary to build leadership capacity for sustained change.

Tests, league tables and statistics

The domination of testing and the importance of improving results adds to the sense of marginalization, leading to a narrowness of focus that can leave staff feeling unable to contribute. For example, when Beverley took up her role in the school, she came with an enthusiasm, expectation and desire that she would play a significant role in the development of the school:

I thought I would work more in a leadership and developmental role but I had a very narrow role, focused to raising SATs results. When David [LEA manager] spoke to me about the position, he said it would be a development role, in which I would work alongside and support teachers. He spoke specifically about you, saying we would work well together. So my expectations were built up and he said that the kind of skills, attributes and experiences I had would complement the way you work.

Beverley believed she came to the school to help build the capacity of teachers and she was clearly resentful of the role she was expected to take on and the agenda she was forced to work towards. She commented:

Your agenda was different; you decided to use me to raise SATs. I did not engage with the skills and experience which I had. I never felt resentful because that was what was demanded of us. It is the external agenda which we have talked about, because it is important to appear successful and success is evaluated in terms of the SATs results.

She was clearly frustrated by this role but had some appreciation of what was happening. While reluctant, she accepted that her role was to raise attainment in SATs, understanding, as I did, that they were a significant measure of our performance. Whether Beverley valued these measures as an indicator of Green Hill's success seemed irrelevant.

I recall a visit from Judy Kugelmass, a professor from the United States, who described such activity as 'playing the game'. Whether the statistics represent a truth, or are part of 'a game' in respect to the improvement of our school is a matter of debate, but what counted is that we had improved our test results and therefore proved our competence. Beverley commented:

We need to ask the question, if the school down the road is getting 80 percent and we get 40 percent, why is it? They do not ask those questions they simply say it should not happen. I think you can have schools in the same neighbourhood with very different intakes. The statistical data agenda puts schools into very simplistic categories, without having any significant understanding of the journeys, contexts, cultures and people. A school 1000 metres down the road can be very different. For example, Green Hill has had years of neglect, what positive benefit is there in comparing us with a school that is stable and successful? I accept that if we do not compare favourably with our statistical neighbours then I will be brought to account. Whether this is fair, reasonable or serves any real purpose I am not sure. Whether the information provides us with an understanding to use for potential improvement is limited. Last year our statistical test data showed over 100 percent improvement, comparable and probably better than 95 percent of the schools in the country. What it tells us about the improvement in the quality of the education we provide is another debate.

Beverley was concerned that test results may be a false indicator of the progress of the school and pupils, but, more significantly, she was concerned that they were given inappropriate attention, at the expense of more important issues within the development of individual children:

Because I think it is done at the expense of other things. If you take my class, where I have total control of their education for a year. I do not think I have created learners, in that they are totally reliant on me for motivation and guidance. I have not extended their self-discipline and capacity to be good learners because of the emphasis we put on the SATs, but it is a brave person who is going to ignore the SATs and focus on the development of self-esteem and self-discipline.

What strikes me here is the word 'ignore'. In our desire to prove ourselves, we were forced into a position that left us neglecting the needs of the children in order for the organization to survive. What Beverley would seem to indicate is that the SATs, school data and inspection process are the starting points for the education we provide for the children within our care. Rather than serving the needs of the children, we were serving the accountability agenda.

Beverley had a clear understanding of where we should be focusing our work and the route that would be most beneficial to the children. I asked her whether she thought we could have achieved our success in SATs by going down a different route.

I think you might have to sacrifice them for a year ... but one thing that has struck me about the children is that once they meet any kind of difficulty, even if it is just mechanical, they give up. Their self-esteem is low and they need a lot of support. The thing about the children is that despite how cocky they behave, underneath the aggression they are so fragile and a misplaced word can throw them. So yes, it is self-esteem, but another thing is their total lack of empathy for other people. They really do not know how to listen and understand other people's point of view. That is evident in the racist, sexist and homophobic comments they make. I have never encountered anything like it, it is horrendous, the throw away comments, which can be really hard-core and done to someone who is upset. They do not understand the impact of their actions on other people.

Beverley did not respond specifically to the question of SATs; rather she expressed values that say we should engage with the individual child. She was clear that we were ignoring our children as people and neglecting some of the fundamental learning skills that would prepare and enable them to lead quality existences. We were never brought to account over such issues. Beverley was particularly emotional when she described the progress of one particular child:

Yes, I am trying to get level fours out of Peter

In response to whether she thought Peter was getting a fair deal she said:

No, because I am exploiting him to get a level four, but I do not feel guilty because that is what he wants. He will judge himself as a success or a failure according to the number of level fours he gets.

While Beverley was sincere in her belief that Peter would be pleased if he got a level four and indicated that she did not feel guilty about this, I found this difficult to accept. Beverley had been a teacher for over 20 years, long before the audit culture started to take hold and become the dominant factor in our lives. On many occasions she had voiced values on education that were contrary to the agenda which she now served. Her starting point was the children, particularly in respect of their needs as learners:

> What I have learned over the last seven or eight years is the decline in a lot of the things we used to value in primary education. In the past you would try to develop study and problem solving skills, which you need to be a true learner. Whereas, what I increasingly do in this school is stand at the front and tell them what they are going to learn and it is all just to pass SATs.

Beverley was adamant that the emphasis on the children as learners was not evident or expected, and that the education Peter received neglected some fundamental rights. As a school, we ignored teaching him some fundamental skills and while, as headteacher, I accept responsibility for that, I take refuge in the fact that I was judged by a system of audit and accountability that did not make demands on such a crucial area of a child's education. The audit system seems to be designed to bring the school to account, judging it by simplistic data measures. What happens to the children within such schools and their day to day education seems to be less important.

In talking about the idea of creating more able learners, Beverley was very conscious of the limitations of the curriculum the children were experiencing in our school:

> Julie [a teacher who had moved on to a school achieving 100 percent success in SATs for the last four years] tells me the school she is now working in, has the same behaviour problems and that it surprised her, but when she told me about the kind of things they do with the children I just think it is bad practice ... They have afternoons doing comprehensions that just ask the children to answer questions. It does not train them to engage in any depth with text, or to love books ... they can decode a piece of text but so what!

Beverley was very determined in her expression of a desire for the children having meaning and a reason to read. She expressed a similar view in relation to writing.

> If you think what they write about, well basically nothing ... Why do you write Andrew? I do not particularly like writing things down but I enjoy it when I have a purpose and an audience to communicate to. These children do not have those. In the past I made lots of big books and stories that were published but it is becoming increasingly difficult to do those kind of things.

In expressing a desire for the children to have ownership of their learning, Beverley made a similar plea on behalf of the teachers:

> We have tried to thematize the curriculum content but we need to go further, we need to be able to decide our own curriculum. For example, at my last school we had a lot of refugee children from Pakistan and so we planned a project about that country. Everything we did was around that. The curriculum was decided in terms of the needs of the children.

As throughout our conversations, Beverley expressed a desire to be involved, to share in the leadership, in partnership with the staff, children and parents and find a way forward for the school. In opposing the accountability agenda, she did so on the grounds that continual inspection creates unnecessary tension and blame; reliance on inspection findings and statistical data may not be the most appropriate evidence to inform about standards; accountability ignores the needs of the individual child and results in an inappropriate curriculum; and that by ignoring the teachers we were limiting the potential to develop necessary leadership capacity.

What we learned

What is evident in the above extracts is that my colleagues had the emotional and intellectually capacity to contribute to the leadership of the school. Sadly, during the period of special measures they were rarely consulted in ways that could have influenced the direction of the school. I suggest that sustainable improvement in a school like Green Hill must start from the knowledge and understandings that already exist within the organization.

It is well documented that educational improvement that is to be long-term can only be achieved when it has the commitment of the people charged with making the change happen. The 'common sense insights' of teachers such as Beverley and Paul indicate what seem to be more promising pathways for sustainable improvement. I suggest that to make use of such expertise requires those in leadership positions to move away from the existing, externally driven bureaucratic, psychological and technical, rational authority, in which teachers are mere technicians responding to the power of audit by continually proving their competence. In moving towards a more professional and moral authority, teachers are more likely to be motivated and emotionally committed to the values and needs of the school. In developing such a leadership capacity, a logical and necessary starting point would be through encouraging teachers to talk about their current situation and what they believe appropriate to bring about necessary changes.

Teachers are in a privileged position in that they have unique access to knowledge about the schools in which they work. Teacher knowledge develops within 'a particular school, school system and society' (Elbaz 1991); they have high context knowledge, compared with people on the outside who have low context knowledge, which involves the use of the common sense insights, for which Waller calls. However, the current national reform agenda does not seem to value such insights and, indeed, can appear to suppress them.

My experience would indicate that policymakers should not ignore the commonsense, contextually rich insights that teachers in urban schools have to offer. I would suggest that these teachers have to be listened to because of the insights they bring and that we should ensure they have the necessary involvement to turn initial, short-term fixes into more meaningful, sustainable improvement.

4

LEADING DEVELOPMENTS IN PRACTICE: BARRIERS AND POSSIBILITIES

Mel Ainscow and Andy Howes

Research points to practitioner inquiry as a strategy for encouraging the development of forms of teaching that can reach out to learners within a class. However, as we saw in the previous chapter, the implementation of such approaches is far from straightforward in school contexts that are facing pressures to improve test and examination results. This chapter describes the experiences of its authors in working in partnership with an urban secondary school to develop more inclusive practices. Their analysis of this experience throws further light on the way contextual factors, particularly those associated with national reform policies, act as barriers to progress. It also suggests some possible ways of addressing these barriers.

It has been argued that progress towards more inclusive education systems requires a fundamental shift in thinking (Skrtic 1991; Ainscow 1999). This involves moves towards what has been described as an 'organisational paradigm' (Dyson and Millward 2000). In general terms, this involves a rejection of explanations of educational failure that concentrate solely on the characteristics of individual children and their families, towards an analysis of the barriers to participation and learning experienced by students within school systems (Booth and Ainscow 2002). In this way, those students who do not respond to existing arrangements come to be regarded as 'hidden voices', who, under certain conditions, can encourage the improvement of schools.

In this chapter we explore some of the practical implications of adopting such a perspective. Specifically, we describe and reflect on the experience of working with one English secondary school in attempting to use evidence to encourage the development of inclusive thinking and practice. This leads us to examine the possibilities and challenges of using such approaches in the realities of schools that are under pressure to raise standards.

Standards and inclusion

We recently completed a three-year study that set out to throw light on how more inclusive practices can be developed in schools (Ainscow et al. 2003a; Ainscow et al. in press). The research was carried out as part of the Economic and Social Research Council's Teaching and Learning Research Programme. The study, which defined inclusive practices as involving attempts to overcome barriers to the participation and learning of students, took the form of an action research network in which teams from three universities worked with groups of schools as they attempted to move practice forward.

Experience in the network supports the findings of earlier research that developments in practice are unlikely to occur without some exposure to what teaching actually looks like when it is being done differently, and exposure to someone who can help teachers understand the difference between what they are doing and what they aspire to do (e.g. Huberman 1993; Little and McLaughlin 1993; Ainscow 1999). More specifically, our research has shown how engaging with various types of evidence can be helpful in encouraging such developments. Evidence can help to create space for reappraisal and rethinking by interrupting existing discourses, and by focusing attention on overlooked possibilities for moving practice forward. Particularly powerful techniques in this respect involve the use of evidence gathered from mutual observation in classrooms and from students about their perceptions of teaching and learning arrangements within a school. We have found that, under certain conditions, such approaches provide *interruptions* that help to 'make the familiar unfamiliar' in ways that stimulate self-questioning, creativity and action.

However, while an engagement with evidence *can* create space for reviewing thinking and practice, it is not in itself a straightforward mechanism for the development of more inclusive practices. The space that is created may be filled according to conflicting agendas. In this way, factors within a school may prevent the experimentation that is necessary in order to foster the development of more inclusive ways of working.

In order to throw light on what this involves we examine in detail what happened in one of the secondary schools in the network. The school was interesting in that, despite the implementation of the sorts of inquiry-based approach we are recommending, progress in relation to the development of inclusive practices was generally disappointing. Reflecting on why this was so draws our attention to the way certain aspects of national policy create barriers to progress. By identifying and analysing the nature of these systemic barriers points to changes that would help to move practice forward in schools.

The account of what happened in the particular school chronicles our struggles as we tried to find a way of integrating the research into the life of the school, which was designated as 'having serious weaknesses' following an inspection. Understandably during the subsequent three years the school was characterized by a sense of tension and uncertainty, particularly during the run-up to a second inspection.

The school is located on a spacious site by a motorway, with a public school type frontage and a mixture of buildings, some in poor condition. In 1996, Ofsted reported that 'nearly 40% of the school's intake came from very socially disadvantaged areas ... the proportion from disadvantaged areas has increased over the last 10 years. The proportion of pupils known to be eligible for free school meals has risen appreciably in recent years and is now above average'. These trends have continued.

The headteacher joined the school in the September prior to the setting up of the network, but the members of the senior management team (SMT) had been there much longer. She explained how, over the years, senior staff had become isolated from processes of teaching and learning, and had spent more time involved in administration. She also explained that there had been 'a culture in the school of hiding underachievement'. Indeed, she talked derisively about the 'caring and sharing' ethos, as opposed to her sense of inclusive leadership, which she characterized as 'caring enough to confront'.

Families in the area tend to prefer their young people to go to a school in a different LEA, or to another nearby high school. Consequently, the school increasingly admitted students from the economically poorer parts of the town, a high proportion of whom were referred to as being from unsupportive homes. Because of its spare places the school also admitted a high number of what were seen as being 'difficult students'.

It was reported that in some lessons, bad behaviour was blamed for the limiting of the curriculum and that some classes were following an impoverished curriculum. The headteacher's overview of the school's key issue was that key stage (KS) 3 teaching and learning was failing students, causing a discipline problem among young people who came to the school without confidence in themselves or the school. A tendency observed and recognized by the staff at the time was to close down educational experience in response to the problems of behaviour. For example, one teacher commented, 'If just two apples slide down to that end, I can't hold it, I have to move to something more *boring*, as the kids would say'.

Developing an agenda

During an early visit to the school we were able to have a detailed discussion with the headteacher and the teacher designated to act as link person, about how the work of our research network might contribute to an overall strategy for improvement. As a result of these discussions we felt reasonably optimistic that we could channel their involvement through the structures that had been set up to lead improvements in teaching and learning. In particular, we felt that it would be possible for us to act as 'critical friends' to those who were leading these initiatives, not least in relation to the collection and analysis of evidence that could be used to develop effective interventions.

At the same time, our optimism was tempered by a series of occasional, private discussions with the head. These helped to provide a better sense of the context and, at the same time, some greater awareness of the tensions that existed within the school. She explained that she had been appointed just over a year previously to 'turn the school round'. However, it had become clear that she would have to address many difficulties if she was to be successful. Already, for example, she had had to exclude six students that term, including one very difficult girl who had become involved in violence during her first morning in the school. During her two-day interview for the job, in May 1999, the head had felt that the school was 'out of control'.

The school was inspected in February 2000 and found to have 'serious weaknesses'. Some LEA staff had suspected that it would be 'placed in special measures'. The report was particularly critical of the senior management team, although not of the head herself. She then set targets for her senior colleagues (for example, 'eliminate trainers in the next three weeks') and discouraged them from 'hiding behind paper'.

We became involved in what the head saw as her strategy for harnessing the enthusiasm for change of the more dynamic staff: the formation of 'school improvement teams'. The members of the teaching and learning team with whom we began to work were volunteers who had responded to an invitation from the head by stating this project as their preference (other teams were focused on projects relating to marketing, primary liaison and behaviour). Most of those who came to the meetings were experienced teachers, three or four having come fairly recently from other schools.

As well as constituting an action group for working on classroom practice, the discussions of this group provided insight into the culture of teaching and learning in the school and some sense of the barriers that existed. So, for example, on one occasion teachers talked about the experience of boys learning from each other what they could get away with, and how others 'popped up' to misbehave when one had been excluded. The point being made was that teachers were finding lessons difficult to cope with, and that these discussions were a place for expressing some of that frustration.

The group of staff met regularly throughout the year to talk about teaching and learning. These discussions were encouraged by engagement with video recordings made of lessons taught by members of the group, and transcripts of interviews with students. Generally the meetings were rather short and hurried, and were not attended by any senior members of staff. Nevertheless, they were well received by those who took part and seemed to lead to interesting discussions.

Towards the end of the first year of our involvement in the school, we reflected on what had happened. Examination results in the previous summer had pointed to some interesting issues. For example, the GCSE results saw an improvement in terms of five A* to C scores, with some 30 percent achieving this level. At the same time, five A to G results were said to be in decline (from 87 to 83 percent), as were the proportion of students achieving A to G (dropping from 93 to 90 percent). In relation to these trends, it had been noted that the school had had some difficulty in appointing appropriately qualified teachers, particularly in maths. There was also a particular problem in so-called 'lower sets' where, apparently, 'weaker' teachers had been required to work.

During the year, we contributed to a residential staff development event for senior and middle management, looking specifically at aspects of leadership and the use of evidence to inform school improvement. We also attended most of the after-school meetings of the teaching and learning group, the members of which seemed to be gaining confidence in using data about their practice. Teachers had verbally shared classroom experiences (good and bad), and interviewed several children about their experience of school. This had led to four members of the group agreeing to have their lessons recorded on video. The first two of these recordings were used at a meeting of the group in order to examine ways of creating forms of dialogue that encourage reflection on thinking and practice, and the sharing of ideas about how colleagues can help one another to make their lessons more inclusive. So, for example, the recording of a modern language lesson focused the group's attention on issues of pace and support for participation, while discussion on a science lesson drew attention to ways in which students can generate their own questions in ways that deepen understanding of subject content. Through these processes the group had been developing a common language to foster a deeper engagement with matters of classroom practice.

Already it was evident that such discussions were beginning to stimulate creativity, while at the same time leading to moments of uncertainty when teachers were confronted with examples of practice that challenged their own experiences and assumptions. We were also finding that it was necessary to set the context in which such discussions could take place, so that those involved recognized that these were not quality assurance and performance management procedures. This was a particular challenge in a school in the throws of post-inspection activities.

Looking to the future, the plan was to continue working on aspects of classroom practice. More colleagues had agreed to have their lessons videoed. During the summer term it was planned to have a half-day with the group, analysing what had been learnt so far and how these lessons might be used during the next year to widen involvement in the school.

Confronting the problem

In fact, the proposed meeting never happened and we became increasingly concerned that our work was becoming even more marginalized. In July we took part in a meeting of the SMT, which by this stage included two newly appointed deputy heads. This followed on from a meeting the previous day when we had explained to the head our frustration at not being able to connect what we were doing to a wider school improvement strategy. As a result of these discussions one of us agreed to formulate a proposal for how to proceed on teaching and learning in the coming school year.

The proposal was based on strategies we had used successfully with colleagues in other schools in the network. It set out to develop an approach to management and leadership that would permeate a focus on learning among *all* members of the school community. It suggested that the academic year 2001–02 would require an intensive and coordinated push in this respect. This would involve a series of interconnected activities, each of which would imply different roles and responsibilities. It went on to propose that all members of the SMT would have to demonstrate their full commitment to the strategy, not least by making time to carry out necessary management and leadership tasks. A key element would involve the regular monitoring of lessons in order to offer support and challenge to teachers. They would also have to work very closely with the heads of those faculties for which they had particular responsibility.

It was also noted that these roles and responsibilities were in themselves challenging and that it would be necessary for the SMT to hold regular meetings in order to share experiences and provide support to one another. As far as possible, we would attend these meetings in order to report on the evidence of their research in the school and to act as critical friends to members of the SMT.

The document went on to spell out in some detail the processes that would be used to encourage activities in all the faculties. These would involve the use of an adapted form of 'lesson study', a systematic procedure for the development of teaching that is well established in Japan and some other Asian countries (Stigler and Hiebert 1999). During the period September to December 2001 a particular approach would be used to kick-start these processes. Following a survey of student views, faculty members would be asked to work in pairs to design a lesson (or series of lessons) to address an aspect of the curriculum that was *not* liked by students or, possibly, staff. They would each teach the lesson, with their colleague observing what happened. Following each observation, the two staff would agree a short commentary on what they had learnt. These commentaries would be presented to meetings of the faculty team. The existing teaching and learning group was to be seen as a resource to faculties as they tried to develop ways of working that would encourage discussion and experimentation.

During the period September to December 2001, little progress was made in respect to the proposed strategy. Despite continued attempts, we failed to make arrangements to attend a further meeting of the SMT. In the meantime, we occasionally joined the meetings of the teaching and learning group. Eventually, with the probability of a second visit by Ofsted looming, it was decided that there should be a meeting of the senior and middle management staff to discuss the development of yet another strategy. This was held on a Sunday afternoon in November 2001. Although this had not been prearranged, one of us chaired the meeting.

Early in 2002 it was announced that the school would be inspected in the second week of March. Meanwhile, it had become clear that yet further staffing changes had disrupted efforts to involve the wider school in action research activities on teaching and learning. At the same time, these changes seemed to offer new possibilities for leadership within an agenda that it was hoped would have more leverage within the school. Specifically, the participation of the school in an Education Action Zone had led to the appointment of a new teaching and learning coordinator, and two advisory teachers in the English and maths departments. There was, however, a strong impression that none of these new staff members had been given much guidance as to their roles and responsibilities.

Yet again, then, we found ourselves facing a new situation and, indeed, new people to link with in relation to our action research activities in the school.

Yet again, things looked hopeful but by now our sense of optimism was tempered by doubt.

In February 2002 we took part in a meeting with the new advisory teachers. Also present were three members of the English department and another teacher representing the teaching and learning group. The exact purpose of the meeting was unclear, as was the reason why these particular people were present. The two English department colleagues talked about the changes in practice that had been stimulated by the introduction of the national KS3 strategy, focusing specifically on the ideas it recommended regarding three-stage lesson formats and the use of lesson objectives. It was apparent that they saw these innovations as very disturbing to their usual ways of working. They also talked about the amount of mutual support the English teachers provided for one another, giving the strong impression that they already did a great deal of collaborative planning. Interestingly, after the meeting one of the advisory teachers mentioned that she had seen no evidence of such collaboration going on.

The two advisory teachers seemed to be developing rather different patterns of work within their respective departments. The one attached to the English department was working on notions of lesson differentiation, focusing mainly on schemes of work and the development of new teaching materials. Her background was in primary education and she was still getting to grips with secondary organization. She was also doing some team teaching. Meanwhile, the advisory teacher working in the maths department suggested that the biggest challenge he faced related to staffing, in that he had found that approximately 70 percent of Year 7 lessons were being taught by non-specialists.

Once again, then, we found themselves in a meeting that lacked purpose and direction. Consequently, yet again we felt forced to provide something of a steer as to what might happen. As a result, it was somehow agreed that during the next few months the work on teaching and learning within the school would concentrate mainly in these two departments, taking advantage of the possibilities raised by the presence of the two advisers. It was also agreed that the meetings of the teaching and learning group would continue, although the links between these two activities were left rather vague.

In relation to the proposed work in the two departments the following questions emerged: how can subject departments improve their practices? What is the role of advisory teachers in such contexts? The assumption was that progress in respect to these two issues, in either or both of these departments, could be used as a means of stimulating similar initiatives in other departments at a later date.

With all of this agreed, it was decided that we would concentrate initially on the English department, partly because of the presence of its staff at the meeting. It was also proposed that the team would try to develop an account of development activities over the next few months, looking to encourage the use of mutual observation and student voices.

Addressing barriers

The difficulties experienced in this particular school continued until the end of the three-year period of our research network funding. They seemed to have emerged from a series of interconnected historical and contextual factors. Together these factors had led to a lack of trust and confidence within the school community, and, as a result, the absence of an authentic strategy for school improvement.

Accounts like this draw our attention to the ways in which external factors, such as inspections, influence and at times constrain the efforts of those in schools to develop their practices. They also illustrate how well-intentioned strategies imposed on schools defined as being in difficulty can work against efforts to move forward on the development of more effective practices. They also point to yet further potential barriers that have to be addressed in order to foster the development of more inclusive practices within schools.

These experiences suggest that while an engagement with evidence can create space for reviewing thinking and practice, it is not in itself a straightforward mechanism for the development of more inclusive practices. The space that is created may be filled according to conflicting agendas. In this way, deeply held beliefs within a school may prevent the analysis and experimentation that is necessary in order to foster the development of more inclusive ways of working.

Such explanations remind us that educational difficulties can so easily be pathologized as difficulties inherent within students. This is true, we suggest, not only of students with disabilities and those defined as 'having special educational needs', but also of those whose socioeconomic status, race, language and gender renders them problematic to particular teachers in particular schools. Consequently, it is necessary to develop the capacity of those within schools to reveal and challenge deeply entrenched, deficit views of 'difference', which define certain types of students as 'lacking something' (Trent et al. 1998).

Specifically, it is necessary to be vigilant in scrutinizing how deficit assumptions may be influencing perceptions of certain students. As Bartolome (1994) explains, teaching methods are neither devised nor implemented in a vacuum. Design, selection and use of particular approaches arise from perceptions about learning and learners. In this respect even the most pedagogically advanced methods are likely to be ineffective in the hands of those who implicitly or explicitly subscribe to a belief system that regards some students, at best, as disadvantaged and in need of fixing or, worse, as deficient and therefore beyond fixing.

Writing about similar processes, Timperley and Robinson (2001) explain how teachers' existing understandings influence the way evidence is interpreted, such that they perceive what they expect to perceive. Consequently, new meanings are only likely to emerge when evidence creates 'surprises'. The role of senior staff is crucial in encouraging such rethinking among their colleagues. So, for example, Lambert and her colleagues seem to be talking about a similar process in their discussion of what they call 'the constructivist leader'. They stress the importance of leaders gathering, generating and interpreting evidence within a school in order to create an 'inquiring stance'. They argue that such information causes 'disequilibrium' in thinking and, as a result, provides a challenge to existing assumptions about teaching and learning (Lambert et al. 1995).

All of this points to the importance of cultural factors in promoting (or inhibiting) student participation. By 'culture' we mean the norms, values and accepted ways of doing things that are reflected in observed practices. Sustaining inclusive educational practice requires an uncompromising commitment to principles of equity among school leaders (Kugelmass and Ainscow 2004). The development of more inclusive approaches does not emerge as a mechanical process in which any one specific organizational restructuring, or the introduction of a particular practice, generates increased levels of participation. Rather, the evidence is that the development of an inclusive culture requires a shared commitment by staff to processes that produce an overall enhancement in participation among all participants.

Given the problematic nature of the notion of culture, it is important to consider what this involves. One aspect of culture seems to be the values and attitudes held by school staff. The extent to which these values include the acceptance and celebration of difference and a commitment to offering educational opportunities to all students, coupled with the extent to which the values are shared across a school staff, relate to the extent to which students actually are enabled to participate. Authentic participation is evident when all students learn alongside others; collaborate in shared learning experiences; actively engage with learning; and have a say in their education. More deeply, participation means being recognized, accepted and valued for oneself (Booth and Ainscow 2002).

Conclusion

Early on in the life of the research network we tried to map out the positions and relationships within our partnerships with the schools. We saw these as involving two, interlinked cycles of action research carried out in partnership by practitioners and researchers. The first of these cycles was driven by the agenda of the partner LEAs and schools, and set out to use existing knowledge within these contexts, supplemented by further research evidence as the means of fostering developments in the field. The second cycle attempted to scrutinize these developments in order to address the overall agenda of the network, using existing theory and previous research, including our own work, as a basis for pursuing deeper understandings. Between the two cycles was a set of boundaries that had to be crossed in order that the two driving agendas could be synchronized.

The story of the secondary school presented in this chapter illustrates the difficulties that can occur as researchers attempt to negotiate this boundary territory with practitioners. Indeed, towards the end of the work, after three years of involvement in that school, one of us wrote about the experience in his research diary, as follows:

Perhaps naively and despite everything that has happened, we remain optimistic about connecting our work to some form of long-term improvement strategy in the school. Getting the issue of inclusion on the agenda remains a problem, although in a wider sense so much of what happens in this school appears to lead to the marginalization of some students and, indeed, some members of the staff.

Within these circumstances, there was considerable evidence of the ways in which groups of students came to be characterized as being largely unteachable by some of the staff. In particular, we saw how the rather complex banding and setting procedures that existed had a strong shaping effect on the perceptions some staff had of certain groups of students. A key issue was, therefore, how could expectations of students in the school be improved? This then related to another question posed by senior staff: how could the views of the school held by the community be improved?

The story reveals how national reform efforts aimed at bringing about improvements in schools that are defined as failing can stimulate what seem to be sensible and well-intentioned improvement efforts, such as the creation of staff improvement groups. Unfortunately, in this instance these moves appeared to add to the sense of failure within the school. Despite lots of discussion and effort, in practice, little progress was made, and some of those involved appeared to be left with a feeling that this was as a result of *their* inadequacies.

The account also raises interesting questions about the roles of researchers in schools. As we have illustrated, in this particular case the unfortunate circumstances that existed over the three years led us to occasionally become involved in ways that we did not intend. In such a context, where roles and responsibilities appear to be uncertain, it is so easy to take on tasks that seem to need doing. Consequently, within the partnership stance we were attempting to adopt we often found ourselves debating whether we should establish clearer and, indeed, safer boundaries.

Nevertheless, there was evidence that within the network the process of collaborative action research helped to develop the research capacity of teachers and, indeed, other staff in participating schools. Often they recognized the value of data that they themselves generated through, for example, engaging with students in conversations, or through observations of classroom and playground behaviour. The regular meetings in the LEAs proved to be helpful occasions for developing a shared language of engagement. But more than this, as members of our research team engaged closely in schools, researching alongside practitioners and sharing findings with one other, the debates in these schools became increasingly grounded in that specific attention which is characterized by research.

Despite the difficulties we have documented here, the work of the network did demonstrate the potential power of collaboration between practitioners and academics as a means of fostering more inclusive practices, although the learning that is necessary in order to take advantage of this potential should not be underestimated. In particular, it requires new forms of relationship between practitioners and researchers, in the way that is outlined by Hiebert et al. (2002). They suggest that fruitful forms of collaboration require a re-orientation of values and goals among both groups. So, they argue, teachers need to move away from the dominant view that teaching is a 'personal and private activity'. Rather, teachers have to adopt the 'more risky view' that it is an activity that can be continuously improved, provided it is made public and examined openly. At the same time, they argue that researchers must stop undervaluing the knowledge teachers acquire in their own classrooms. In this way researchers will be able to recognize the potential of 'personal knowledge as it becomes transformed into professional knowledge' (Hiebert et al. 2002).

Our own experience suggests that successful practitioner/researcher part-nerships involve a complex social process within which colleagues with very different experiences, beliefs and methodological assumptions learn how to live with one another's differences and, even more difficult, learn how to learn from these differences. It also suggests that, where appropriate condi-tions exist, such partnerships can help to facilitate school-level processes that lead to more inclusive practices. Later chapters address the question of how such conditions might be created.

ACHIEVING SUSTAINABLE IMPROVEMENTS IN URBAN SCHOOLS

Mel West, Mel Ainscow and Jacqui Stanford

So far we have presented accounts that demonstrate how national policies can inhibit the potential of urban schools to bring about improvements in their practices. At the same time, these accounts have pointed to the potential of the knowledge and expertise that exists within the schools. How, then, can school leaders create the conditions that will make better use of this potential in order to achieve sustainable improvement in such schools? With this in mind, this chapter analyses the strategies used within a group of secondary schools that have succeeded in increasing and sustaining attainment levels over time in order to learn more about the factors that are associated with their success. The evidence presented does not lead to a 'recipe'. Rather it suggests that the most appropriate way forward is to focus on determining the right sort of 'ingredients', mixed to suit the contexts and circumstances of individual schools.

Over the last 15 years or so, the range of policies aimed at raising standards in English schools has broadened. In particular, the introduction of performance targets has brought greater pressure to increase levels of attainment among students, especially at 16 plus, where national GCSE examination results offer a yardstick that allows some aspects of school performance to be compared. However, despite continuing, if modest, gains in overall attainment levels, there remain a number of schools, typically but not exclusively schools in difficult urban contexts, where progress has been difficult to secure.

Yet there are schools that appear to demonstrate that it is possible to break out of the cycle of low expectations and low attainment. These are schools facing challenging circumstances that have succeeded in increasing and sustaining attainment levels over time. This chapter focuses on such schools. Specifically, it examines progress in a sample of English secondary schools in which progress has been sustained in order to learn more about factors that are associated with success.

The study

The study was carried out on behalf of the Department for Education and Skills (DfES). It looked at 34 secondary schools where the proportion of students attaining five GCSE passes at grades A to C in 1997 was below 20 percent, that is, schools where attainment was well below the national average. All were schools that had seen steady (and for the most part year on year) improvements in this proportion over the subsequent six years. In some cases, progress had been spectacular; in a few schools attainment levels reached and even moved above the national average.

Our purpose was to investigate the strategies used in these schools and to tease out lessons that might help leaders in schools still struggling to locate strategies for sustained improvement. To this end, the headteachers in the 34 schools were interviewed about what they and their colleagues in the school had done, and about what it was, in their view, that had 'made the difference'.

There were 23 males and 11 females in the group. Only three of the heads could be classed as recent appointments: one of these had been in post for 18 months, another for 30 months and the third for four years. The average length of appointment was seven years, with the longest serving head having been in post for ten years. For all but one of the heads this was their first headship.

Of course, any such study has limitations. So, for example, it should be remembered that the findings we report here are only drawn from headteachers' perspectives. Indeed, it would be very interesting to learn more about the perceptions of others within these schools. Also, in seeking 'generalizations' and 'lessons' that may transfer, we were aware that the more successful a school is, the less the school becomes a practical model to be imitated by others (Glickman 2003). Above all, we were aware that it is the first steps that are most difficult to take (see, for example, Myers 1996; Reynolds 1998) and that, looking back through the lens of hindsight, headteachers may not recall exactly what it was that moved the school onto its upward trajectory. Nevertheless, we believe that the accounts we collected do provide important insights into processes of improvement, and offer instructive analyses of the kinds of thinking and action needed in schools facing challenging circumstances.

Perceptions of the task

Many of the heads indicated that the main catalyst for improvement was fear of school closure brought on by falling rolls, a history of poor performance in examinations, and the impact of negative local press coverage on the image of the school. Indeed, they felt that these pressures from outside had provided helpful levers for change, even though they often had a darker side.

Headteachers were keen to argue that improving exam results is not the same as improving the quality of schooling. In this respect there was considerable reference to the strategic and, sometimes, moral dilemmas they faced in relation to their improvement efforts. In particular, they talked of tensions they had experienced between the need to raise standards, as measured by aggregate test and examination scores, and their concern as educators to focus on the needs of all of their students. So, for example, one head explained:

> Two years ago, although our A to C scores weren't impressive, our five A to Gs were over 90 percent. ... So, last year we put more effort into the five A to Cs and our five A to G rate dipped. Actually, we saw this as a bit of a failure. No one really noticed and actually we got all these congratulations for the big improvements.

In talking about this concern about inclusion, some heads drew attention to more worrying effects, not least being an increase in student exclusions. For example:

> People think that when you are improving exam results that it will necessarily improve the quality of schools, and I think in many cases it does. But I think one of the consequences for us has been that there has been a fantastic increase in exclusions

The heads also talked about a series of challenges that they had had to face in order to move their schools forward. Many felt that the most significant of these was related to the need to raise the expectations of staff, students and parents. One head talked about 'making students believe in themselves, when they and their parents doubt or don't have good expectations of their academic ability'. The same person referred to the need to challenge the 'what do you expect' culture among some teachers. Another head commented:

> You see, staff and students were down-trodden; the school had been slated in the national and local press. My challenge was to raise their self-esteem and self-image, which is not an overnight job ... There were hard decisions about having to release people because we were over-staffed, to tell people they are not good enough for the job. All of those things were challenges, but nothing compared to changing the ethos of a community that didn't think that it was any good and didn't have any right to be any good

Some of the heads also faced significant difficulties when it appeared that their own expectations clashed with those of parents. For example:

> Challenging parents' perceptions was really difficult because I came in with, you know, a clear view of the school and a very clear view of where I wanted it to be. What I didn't expect, that the parents didn't want it to change. ... They were quite comfortable with the cosy school.

This need to raise expectations by challenging existing values and beliefs left some headteachers anxious about possible implications for people's lives. They were conscious that their efforts were adding further pressure on staff, pupils and parents who were already under stress. Commenting on these worries, one head said:

The regime in schools has changed ... Especially for the kids who come from extremely deprived backgrounds, such as ours, that can have greater consequences than in other [circumstances] ... The school agenda is different from the children's and parents'. The stress that this brings to children and their parents is significant in some cases. Sometimes, the parents and the child would prefer not to have to deal with that stress, beg us to move their child down a set, unhappy about the extra work lessons and the extra homework. I hadn't appreciated, really, the extent to which there was stress in their lives normally ... Many of those young people's lives and families are lived in terrible, terrible stress. It's not just a matter of teaching the kids. It's almost caused a change in the whole family's approach to what education is about.

It is here that we see one of the limitations of the study, of course. The data we have give no clue to how these efforts to change expectations were regarded by others within these school communities. We are left reflecting, for example, are these explanations masking what were, perhaps, perceived as processes of bullying?

Related to the importance of raising expectations, most of the heads saw the need to get their colleagues to set appropriate targets as the second most significant challenge they faced. Mostly, they saw this in terms of expectations during lessons. Indeed, many talked of the challenge of making sure that there was a continuous emphasis on the improvement of teaching and learning. Talking about this, one head explained that here 'teachers wanted to do good for the kids, but ... didn't quite realize that the kids could stand a bit more rigour'. Linked to this emphasis on teaching and learning, was the challenge of getting children to work outside of the classroom on academic tasks and activities.

Issues to do with the wider context of the school also posed significant challenges for many headteachers. For example, some talked about the pressures brought about because their schools were surrounded by selection systems that 'creamed off the best students'. Many of the schools faced falling rolls because of their poor image in the community, and most felt vulnerable to receiving the least able and most difficult children under local admission arrangements. Some of the schools were surrounded by areas of significant social deprivation, indeed, one head referred to a 'drugs and guns culture'. Many needed urgent improvements in the quality of their physical environments and, in some cases, there were also difficulties arising from split-site operations.

The recruitment and retention of staff posed particular challenges for some heads, especially where schools were known to be in difficulty and in areas where living costs are high. The labels of 'special measures' or 'serious weaknesses' tended to add to such difficulties. Some heads linked these difficulties to issues of funding. One argued that 'schools such as this are not funded appropriately'. Another felt that 'fragile funded projects are not particularly helpful', and that 'the strings attached' may inhibit schools' ability to respond appropriately to local issues and concerns. Commenting further, the same head explained, 'We incorporate very positively these government initiatives, but quite often they stymie and restrict what you want to do'.

Effective strategies

In general terms, four interconnected strategies were identified by a majority of the heads as being the most successful in raising achievement in the schools. These related to: changing the culture of the school; focusing on teaching and learning; reviewing the school day; and the purposeful use of data. At the same time, many of the headteachers were keen to explain that no one strategy could be regarded as the reason why their schools had improved. For example, one head stated:

> I changed a thousand things to do with the school by 1 percent. Now I think we spend more time improving one thing 1000 percent. The list goes on forever. Because if you're talking about raising standards the list goes to the toilet brushes, the cleaning, the food the children eat, the way staff conduct themselves. The list is endless really.

Most of the heads talked in detail about their efforts to change what they saw as being the culture of their schools. They mainly described these efforts in terms of changing values and beliefs. This involved building relationships, strengthening morale and raising expectations. Here it was rather noticeable that there was a concern for staff to distance themselves from notions of 'caring for' their pupils. There was a determination among the headteachers to assert that their schools' business was the education of children, enabling them to meet the criteria of success as recognized nationally. Interestingly, this emphasis was even evident among the few that maintained that they focused on caring for the child.

A careful reading of what the heads actually said during the interviews suggests that, in fact, many schools *had* increased their emphasis on what might be considered to be social needs. It struck us that, perhaps, this apparent contradiction arose from their concern to convey the extent to which they privileged teaching and learning as *the* focus of their schools. In practice, many of the strategies intended to build relationships, morale and expectations, appeared to be strongly linked to this overall focus on teaching and learning. In this sense, the concern to foster social and emotional development can be seen as a necessary feature of successful teaching.

The focus on improving teaching and learning was seen by many of the heads as also being closely related to the needs of staff. This included a requirement to redefine roles and responsibilities such that there were new interpretations of working relationships, management arrangements, teams and duties among both senior staff and teachers. Headteachers specifically tried to ensure that they were able to appoint teachers of the highest quality who were suited to the school. This also meant that those who were not perceived to be willing to take on necessary changes would be encouraged to 'move on'.

There was also a striking appreciation of the need to support teachers and, indeed, other staff, so as to enable them to operate successfully. Many of the heads were concerned to create 'a happy place' to work, 'a place where they [staff] would want to be', not least because recruitment and retention posed such difficulties. In the same way, some heads encouraged their staff to take a similar view in relation to the pupils. In particular, they explained that they wanted teachers who would spend time talking to the pupils, both formally and informally. Indeed, this emphasis on talking to and listening to students was seen as a key strategy for school improvement. It was hardly surprising, therefore, that many of the heads saw this as something of a priority in relation to their own use of time. One head explained, 'If the kids know that you are listening and are acting on what they say, it makes a significant difference to their attitudes to school'. She added, 'It's also useful as a lever for challenging staff attitudes'.

Some heads also talked about the importance of fostering the teachers' professionalism such that they knew that their expertise was respected and that they were trusted to conduct themselves in the best interests of the students. Emphasis was placed on developing systems that allowed members of staff to teach without interruptions. At the same time, strategies were used to challenge teachers to think about their ways of working. Here, target setting and engagement with data were seen as being particularly important. Research evidence was used in some schools to develop teachers' understandings of how children learn. What we see, then, is evidence of a balanced use of pressure and support. Although in these schools more strategies were directed at challenging teachers than at supporting them.

Targets for individual pupils and the school in general were linked to the choice of appropriate courses. So, for example, schools offered applied GCSEs, and a range of other vocational courses. Modular courses were also taken on where they were deemed to be more appropriate for some pupils. Here, of course, there is just a hint of the 'rationing' referred to by Gilborn and Youdell (2000) as a strategy for focusing greater attention on those students who are seen to be more likely to achieve the required standards in examinations.

Easter and summer schools seemed to be increasingly common in these schools. Easter residentials, in particular, have become a popular method of intensive preparation of examination groups. Many of the schools also put on a wide range of extra-curricular activities, including sessions directed at the completion of homework and/or course work. These activities were implicated, in the reviewing of the school day and the redrafting of timetables, in order to maximize teachers' use of time. For some of the schools there did not seem to be enough hours in the school day to fit in all the extra courses, the additional options and the various workshops aimed at raising attainment.

The use of data was seen by all of the heads as a key factor in the improvement of teaching and learning, the curriculum and the culture and image of the school. Of course, the way that data are used is vital in this respect. For example, one head commented that this was about:

> Develop[ing] a climate where people believed [that] what they were doing was having an effect – data was very useful here, target-setting – and also changing expectation, demonstrating progress. The value-added measures were crucial; then you could talk to students and show it to inspectors.

Data were also used to agitate for improvement while at the same time appearing to be non-threatening. For example:

I also have a tactic that I use with the teaching staff where I can read off data on GCSE results which shows how pupils have performed in an individual subject and how that same group of children has performed across all the other subjects. And then I can say to a head of department, you are half a grade or a grade below in your subject. And then if they say to me, 'Well, I don't get the best pupils', I say to them, 'No, you may not, but still looking at the same group of children, they have achieved better in other subjects, so there are questions about yours'.

Data were also seen as a means by which the heads could demonstrate and, indeed, celebrate achievements:

scores tell us what the kids should be getting, [this] meant that the teachers could see what they were doing and that was crucial. Staff could see some recognition and the value they had added, which was a very good thing for them ... giving staff the confidence to take risks.

Being radical

During the interviews, headteachers were asked if they felt that any of their strategies were 'radical' in any sense. Most seemed very reluctant to embrace this description, noting that what was needed were 'essentially common-sense' approaches. For example:

When I looked at your list [interview schedule], I was desperately looking for something that I could say something radical about. I'm not radical. The school isn't radical. We just worked really hard.

Another headteacher attempted to shed some light on the unease:

I don't think so. It's down to what are good operational practices for any workplace. You could say that redrafting the timetable for a day is radical; I don't think it is. The word 'radical' to me tends to suggest ... the fact that somebody or some idea can change things overnight. I don't think they can.

Strategies that might be considered radical seemed to coalesce around arrangements for teaching: the extension of the teaching day including extra curricular activities; Saturday classes; changing the teaching day to suit the children; redrafting the timetable for a day; and vertical tutor groups.

Four headteachers did feel that they had used radical strategies. One talked about changing the school's admissions policy: taking in more students. Extending the school day was also mentioned by one head. Commenting on other possible 'radical' developments, a headteacher observed that: 'We decided we're going to have a good time; we're going to have fun'. For another, the fact that 'there is a common understanding of targets which relate to the individual child, are simple and are used throughout the whole school is quite radical'. Another spoke of a 'radical curriculum' that ensured a 'rich and diverse provision at Key Stage 4 ... [so that] students had maximum opportunity to build on their interests and have access to a whole range of vocational courses as well as GCSEs'. This same headteacher also highlighted as radical the practice of students being involved in research in the school, alongside university researchers and LEA staff. Together they analysed data from examination results, and also teaching and learning styles. The findings of such research were then used within staff development activities.

On balance, then, the headteachers in this study did not characterize their actions as radical, preferring to describe what had been achieved in terms of common approaches pursued systematically. However, the fact remains that these apparently simple measures were not previously in place – perhaps their introduction rather than their substance could be considered radical in these contexts. This is an issue that requires more detailed and more carefully contextualized accounts.

Sustainable improvement

In the main, the headteachers attributed the success that their schools had enjoyed to the hard work of staff and students. Once the hard work started to effect positive changes, most found that 'success breeds success', and early successes, in particular for new headteachers, were significant in improving and maintaining achievements.

One head explained, success became 'a big loop that feeds back on itself . . . Very difficult to get going' but 'once on a roll it becomes easier'. Another argued that it is 'a virtuous cycle [that] is self-perpetuating . . . Now we haven't got the battles that we had. The critical mass is with us'.

It seems that with success in motion, a 'feel-good' factor becomes present that strengthens staff and pupil confidence to achieve more. Expectations are raised, and this seems to underpin improvements. One head suggested that for the staff in these schools, 'the past is scary' and they 'can't afford to go back to square one'. Success, on the other hand, generates visible, measurable returns in terms of the school's possibilities:

> Once on a roll it becomes easier, not necessarily in terms of rigour that the staff give to it, but in the quality of the in-take of course. Having got your results up and parents having confidence in the school leads to higher attainers joining the school . . . The 6th form becoming academic, not a small vocational offer, giving the kids something to reach for, and seeing the students picking up A levels and going on to university, pushes the brighter ones into doing well.

Headteachers explained that they had used every opportunity to celebrate positive achievements. This involved 'making sure everybody feels good about themselves' and that 'the students feel part of the success'. One head talked of a commitment to 'working in the tradition of success: very formal achievement evenings, celebrities in, parties, press cuttings, showing that successes are valued'.

All the heads felt that the leadership team has an important and significant role in protecting and building on past achievements. They must lead in acknowledging the hard work of staff and pupils as well as the eventual successes. It is crucial that they keep both the staff and the pupils 'on board', ensuring that all staff and pupils know the current vision, direction and strategies of the school as it develops. Leadership also needs to be at the centre of strategies to project and protect the ethos of the school. This includes valuing the staff and pupils, encouraging 'friendly' competition among them, keeping the focus on teaching and learning, with attention to detail and rigorous monitoring, reviewing and evaluation. The performance management of teachers needs to be underpinned by a commitment to continuing professional development for all teachers and thoughtful induction for new teachers to the schools. Teachers need to feel supported and allowing flexibility in their teaching arrangements seems a significant way to show them support.

It is also the task of the leadership team to ensure that new avenues and opportunities for the school are explored. In particular, it is important to establish the principle that other people's ideas are welcomed and valued, and, for example, that the school development plan belongs to everybody in the school. At the same time, the school, and specifically the leadership team, has to ensure 'you don't stand still', are 'turning attention to those other things that are not yet hitting the mark' and 'focusing on each year group, constructing a programme for them within the overall ethos of improvement'.

The heads argued that the use of data had become an increasingly important way of sustaining progress. While schools are clearly very data-rich, there is evidence of them recognizing the need 'to be discriminating on target-setting; there's so much data around these days, so it is a question of which data give the best predictions'. The schools had become more adept at using data to supplement national test results with their own internal assessments – and at trusting their own data more as they 'build up a historical data-base' on the profiles of the schools' particular students. In this way, target setting had become a systematic means of maintaining progress by encouraging both staff and students to set and check on progress towards short-term goals.

While the contribution of the leadership team is clearly vital, many of the heads also looked to middle management as an 'engine for change'. For example, one head suggested, 'Results come from the subject departments, so it is making sure that middle management is strong and supports those working within those departments. Sustainability has come through working with departments'.

In thinking about sustainability, some of the heads emphasized the importance of retaining a hardcore of teachers. This is necessary, they argued, to safeguard the consistency of approach within the school. Of course, teacher retention is also important because recruitment can be an issue for schools in challenging circumstances. One head explained:

And, in terms of sustainability, some of the pressures of inner city schools make people reluctant to apply to us. So it's not just the social context, because many teachers will put up with that. What they are worried about is, 'Is this school vulnerable? Will I get inspected every two years? Will I be criticized because my lessons are not up to scratch when I know that I am having to work really hard with families with beha-viourally challenged children?' And the pressure in terms of judging us in exactly the same way as schools in more affluent areas are judged. That is going to militate against getting the really good teachers into our schools.

Heads felt that staff must feel truly involved in the decisions made and the activities going on in the school, and given responsibilities that make them feel challenged. Supporting and motivating staff through acknowledgement and celebration of their work promotes their sense of being valued. Feedback to teachers needs to be honest both on good and on less favourable features of their work, as this is an important part of sustainability. Teachers also need space to take risks, experiment and seek ways to 'reinvent the wheel' in the quest to find the best ways to teach the children in their charge. These efforts need to be set within a context where teaching and learning matters have a high profile, and pupil input is encouraged, such that pupils see themselves as partners in learning and are prepared to extend themselves as well.

It was notable, too, that many headteachers spoke about the 'constant pressure' that was placed on students to ensure that they met their targets. There was admission that 'the pressure is intense ... The boys have nowhere to hide ... We know unless we keep the pressure on we're not going to achieve'. Further, 'if you are being taught the same way all the time, you're not going to be an effective learner. Things going on after school, Easter classes ... all put in the melting pot means that there is quite a varied way of learning your stuff. That does keep the motivation going'. These strategies also provided important avenues for students to gain new experiences, which furthered their motivation to achieve and increased their expectations.

Drawing the lessons

So, then, what are the implications for policy and practice in the field? In particular, what does this study suggest about the ingredients that need to be incorporated into improvement strategies?

All but one of those interviewed were in their first headship and had been appointed to schools confronted by a bewildering range of difficulties. While these difficulties were generally understood within the school, and sometimes (for example, in the case of special measures) had been signalled clearly to the wider community, practical plans to address the difficulties had not, in most cases, been developed. Indeed, it seems that while understanding the diffi-culties is a vital precursor to the development of effective strategies for dealing with them, this very understanding can in itself become a dis-empowering force. When the full list of problems has been drawn up, and staff members are able to enumerate the many barriers to progress, simply contemplating these can paralyse even the most enthusiastic of teachers. Consequently, in the heads' descriptions of the circumstances from which they started, we note a sense of helplessness that needs to be overcome before progress is possible. Our feeling is that the first, important achievement of these heads was to move the school community on, beyond this 'help-lessness', into the realization that things could change. The ways heads went about this, inevitably, varied from school to school.

Of course, any study of this kind must attempt to identify common ele-ments, as it seeks to identify the ingredients that combine into success. However, useful as it is to know what these ingredients are, it is equally important to recognize that they do not readily come together into any one 'recipe' that will transform the school. We therefore feel that a note of caution is necessary here. Yes, there do seem to be common ingredients, but these need to be mixed in different proportions and added in a different order according to the school's circumstances. This suggests that possibly the most important attribute of a headteacher in a school facing challenging circum-stances is an ability to analyse the context as quickly as possible, as suggested by Harris and Chapman (2002).

Thus, for example, it is clear that focusing on teaching and focusing on learning are both important, and that once the school is into a cycle of improvement, both are kept under regular evaluation and review. However, whether to start from teaching and progress to its impact on learning, or to begin by looking at learning and then explore the implications for teaching, needs to be considered in context. A school with a static and exhausted teaching force (as one head described them: 'down-trodden' by the daily challenges and disappointments) is unlikely to respond to having current practices placed under the microscope, but may be engaged by looking at the learning needs and problems of the pupils. Conversely in a school with relatively inexperienced, junior teachers and poor subject leadership, staff may respond very positively to measures which focus on teaching approaches that can reduce the number of classroom problems they are encountering.

Similarly, 'controlling behaviour' is a common thread. However, in some schools, this had been (successfully) tackled by isolating certain behaviours and targeting them. In others, behaviour had been addressed in a more general context as a facet of culture or relationships within the school. In some behaviour had been improved, not by a focus on behaviour itself, but by focusing on those activities and approaches that engage students in learning. Thus, while we can see that behaviour management is always associated with raising attainment in difficult schools, how this issue is addressed needs to be carefully calibrated to match with the history and context of the particular school.

There were similar variations in the approaches used to boost self-esteem and expectations (among staff and students) in the ways schools had engaged with and won over their communities, and in the methods used to identify progress and celebrate success. Our feeling, therefore, is that the strategies and approaches that have been highlighted in the previous section need to be seen as a bank of ideas that may help headteachers to develop their own actions plans for their own circumstances; they are not a 'list' of things to do.

Concluding remarks

Collectively then, these schools demonstrate what look to be indications of promising progress in relation to sustainable school improvement. However, they also reveal a rich variety of pathways that have been followed. While the problems confronting such schools may be common, solutions tend to be individual and context-specific. In the same way, the opportunities grasped are also varied. It was clear, for example, that the schools had each reached different conclusions about which of the many government schemes and initiatives available would best support their efforts to raise standards. It was also evident that the choices made have influence that spreads beyond the particular 'initiative', as other school priorities and plans are wrapped around the selected pathway.

Our impression here is that, increasingly, English schools *are* finding pathways to diversity within the government's framework for reform. Despite some understandable grumbling about the number of policies and initiatives, and the pressures these have placed on schools and teachers, it does seem that the range of opportunities has, in the case of these schools at least, offered a degree of freedom to plan their own futures and to plot their own routes. Undoubtedly, the fact that there has been a range of levers for improvement, and that increased autonomy at school level to decide which levers to pull comes with improved performance, has been important to their success. It seems that when schools accept that improvement is possible, and they decide consciously and deliberately to achieve this, progress follows. It is when staff recognize that collectively they *are* able to influence student achievement, that they find opportunities for development within the current policy framework.

6

CONFOUNDING STEREOTYPES: RISK, RESILIENCE AND ACHIEVEMENT IN URBAN SCHOOLS

Helen M Gunter

This chapter reports on a study undertaken in six secondary schools in a large metropolitan LEA in England. The LEA had identified that within these schools students were achieving against the odds. A small-scale qualitative evaluation based on in-depth interviews with students, teachers and leaders was designed to gather the experiences of learning and school life in general. The emphasis was on describing the positive features of practice, and the self-reported reasons for success in building capacity for learning within the school. The research shows that while there are risk factors that increase the likelihood of underachievement, they are not determinants of underachievement. A crucial factor in these six schools is the importance of professionality making the difference through educational leadership as a relational practice.

The account of this study begins with a conceptualization of what might be termed the *achievement paradox*. The purpose of schools and schooling is to enable all pupils to achieve appropriate and meaningful goals, yet the measurement of attainment focuses on quantifiable outcomes across a pre-scribed range of subjects and courses. So, on the one hand, teachers engage with pupils to promote learning, experience pupil dispositions towards learning and see how factors (social, economic, cultural) that impact on learning have to be responded to and accommodated in context. On the other hand, teachers have to implement non-negotiable, externally determined categorizations and measurements of achievement underpinned by an approach to pedagogic and leadership processes that classifies pupils in ways that do not always connect with their needs and identities.

This chapter provides ideas, evidence and arguments about how such contradictions can be worked through in practice and in particular, underlines the need for those in the education community to rethink their positions on what is meant by 'achievement' or by 'underachievers'. In rejecting the influence of external and inappropriate metrics on teachers' practice, I argue that schools as communities do not primarily exist outside of the people who create, sustain and recreate them everyday. Within such communities, successful learning relationships are based on dependency, without complacency. Dependency is productive, because it is about enabling the cognitive and affective security necessary for risk-taking within authentic learning relationships.

The achievement paradox

The current discourse regarding pupil achievement in compulsory education is around the measured benefits of schooling at particular key stages. Abstracted national standards have been created, such as the measure of five A* to C grades at the end of KS4, and levels of achievement are identified through the aggregation of statistics at different levels: individual, through targets and progress monitoring; groups (e.g. gender, class, ethnicity), through patterns of statistics tracking differences in outcomes; teachers, through the value they have added to individual and group scores; and schools (as a whole or within departmental or subject subunits), through their overall impact on pupil outcomes. Statistical analyses are used to show how individual, group and organizational achievement has been delivered through increases on baseline (or entry into a school or a programme) scores. As all pupils have the potential to achieve, a failure to do so is a systemic matter. If the 'system' is working properly, underachievement can be rectified or prevented. Remedial strategies can be targeted through categorization of students: first, based on, for example, ethnicity, gender, whether they have special needs, are children in care, are traveller children, or have teenage mothers; second, based on areas of economic, social and political disadvantage, such as inner cities and/or large areas of social housing; and, third, based on areas of performance, through comparisons with other national states in relation, for example, to numeracy and literacy scores.

Categorization can enable patterns regarding achievement to be identified and support to be targeted in an efficient and effective way. Such reasoning features strongly within, for example, debates about single sex classes and schools, and the segregation of African-Caribbean boys for teaching. These approaches are highly contested, not least because categorization is constructed and mediated through practice. In reality, educational professionals are working in ways that reveal the complexity of those who are grouped and counted, and at the same time strive to give recognition to individual experiences of educational interventions (Smyth 2005). There are important tensions – if children are identified as failing, then we need to ask in relation to what? Who decides that five A* to Cs is an appropriate outcome, whose aspirations are constructing pupils' (and teachers') lives in this way, and for what purpose? It is clear from research that not only teachers, but also pupils have been 'an absent presence' (Ball 1997: 241) in educational reform. Yet, as the objects of that reform, it is their lives that have been 'tidied up' through the imposition of performance measurement systems. Target setting and monitoring have replaced the reality of lived lives, and the attraction of this is our need to be seen to be in control of educational performance. For Fielding

(2001), target setting, 'is, in one sense, the Viagra of economic and educational underperformance: set some targets and you'll feel better, be seen to get something done and satisfy the prurience of an increasingly promiscuous accountability' (2001: 143).

A necessary distinction needs to be made between underachievement and underachievers. While the former is a situation that anyone may find himself or herself in, the latter is a label attached to a group that can stereotype and be negative both as an experience and as a practice. Gillborn and Mirza (2000) illuminate this point:

> Differences in average achievement between social groups raise cause for concern but do not, in themselves, prove anything about the potential of those groups. The reasons for such relative 'underachievement' are multiple and patterns of inequality are not fixed. For example, here and in previous Ofsted review of the field, evidence shows that any one group, say African-Caribbeans, may be ranked poorly in national measures of achievement (such as the proportion attaining five higher grades (A*–Cs) in their GCSE examinations), but the same group can be doing relatively well in some schools and in some LEAs.
>
> (2000: 7)

Here, attention needs to be given to the exercise of agency on the one hand and the structuring context in which categorization is located on the other, and questions can be asked about why particular individuals, groups, schools and initiatives interact in ways that challenge the general patterns. Consequently, examining education within an urban context does not identify location simply as a backdrop to the playing out of local and national interventions, but rather as a site where educational reform is being actively constructed through practice. Then labels can be challenged not only by researchers asking pertinent questions, but also by pupils themselves who resist and challenge the toxic identities that the labels can create (Lauria and Mirón 2005). A focus on social interactions in context means that identity is authored through what Holland and Lave (2001) argue is 'dialogic' – a struggle over open-ended meanings: 'dialogism insists upon the always-engaged-in-practice, always-engaged-in-dialogue, unfinished character of history in person' (2001: 18). This requires an approach to describing and understanding social interactions that is less concerned with cause and effect, but seeks to reveal and analyse risk, resilience and capability.

All pupils are at risk of failing to reach the achievement yardstick. Teachers intentionally place pupils in situations where achievement is expected, and in recognizing that there are structures that can enable or limit achievement we can focus on the nature of the risk. For children from middle-class homes (Ball 2003) the risk is not so great as the cultural capital of home and school are complementary (for example, books, language, rules and culture). Yet for other children the stakes may be high because not only what goes on in school but also the purposes and value of schooling may be disconnected from the ways they construe their lives. Practitioners need to know about how agency is exercised and about how structures challenge its resilience. This is essential, because it enables interventions at individual, group, school or systemic level to be sufficiently differentiated not to simply remediate but to build individual capability.

Sen (1999: 18) argues for 'the expansion of the "capabilities" of persons to lead the kind of lives they value – and have reason to value', and so there is a need to acknowledge the way the exercise of choice and agency is experienced by pupils in schools. He also talks about a 'capability set' and the 'freedom to achieve' or 'the alternative functioning combinations from which this person can choose' (1999: 75). He focuses on choice, and underlines that 'it is possible to attach importance to having opportunities that are *not* taken up' (1999: 76). The exercise of agency has been described by Nussbaum (1999) through the identification of, first, *basic capabilities* such as aptitudes and abilities; second, *internal capabilities* which enable readiness through education and training; and, third, *combined capabilities* where the internal and external interrelate through institutional and legal structures that enable and constrain actions. She goes on to argue that all three need attention: having ability needs to be supported by a readiness to act, and needs external structures to legitimize and enable. When looking at pupils at risk of underachievement, a recognition of the complex interrelationships that create, sustain and destroy individual capabilities can provide us with a valuable, additional perspective.

Challenging stereotypes

The case study LEA had identified a general achievement gap for African-Caribbean pupils; Pakistani and Bangladeshi heritage pupils; white boys in disadvantaged areas; children in public care; and children with special needs. The approach by the LEA was to recognize that not all children in these groups underachieved, but that they were more at risk of underachievement. A range of interventions was in place. However, data showed that within some schools, pupils were less at risk of underachievement, and the LEA wanted to know what was happening in these schools and whether there were strategies in place that could support similar pupils in other schools in the city.

A total of 30 students, 8 senior managers and 10 middle managers/teachers were interviewed, and relevant documents (for example, Performance and Assessment/Panda reports) were examined. The emphasis was on making visible the subjective perceptions of those involved in the schools, so that their experiences of developing good practice could be acknowledged. Additionally it might suggest how resilience within the lived lives of learners and their teachers can overcome risk factors and stereotyping.

The schools

A review of documentation shows that the number of children:

- receiving free school meals was above the national average in all six schools;
- with English as an additional language was very high in four of the schools;
- defined as having special educational needs was above the national average in three of the schools;
- attending was below the national average in five of the schools.

As one headteacher noted, 'the situation is very complex, and I have always argued that school improvement is context specific ... you have to find what works at a given time, in given circumstances'. Poverty is regarded as the key barrier to achievement, as one head of department noted, 'the children get physically tired here'. Cultural capital is low because studying is not a part of the regularities of everyday life.

One school raised the issue of the movement of pupils into and out of schools as having a significant impact on achievement, with 35 per cent of Year 11 who had not started in Year 7, and so the combined effect of low socioeconomic status and high mobility makes underachievement more likely. Another school raised the issue of criminality, when the headteacher talked about how there is 'an alternative society ... they have a party for the first court appearance, are congratulated on their first sentence, and many boys hover between this society and the moral code presented in school'.

Despite this context there is ample evidence of achievement:

- In four schools key stage 3 scores were above the national average when compared with schools in similar circumstances, with three out of the four well above the national average;
- In five schools those pupils with five or more A* to C grades were at least broadly in line with national averages in comparison with schools in similar contexts. In five of the schools the pupils with five or more A* to G grades were at least broadly in line with national averages in comparison to schools in similar contexts. In all six schools the one or more A* to G grades were above the national average in comparison with others schools in similar contexts;
- Pupils in all six schools made average or above average progress (value added) when compared with pupils nationally;
- Ofsted reported that all six schools were making a difference, with positive features noted such as leadership and management, high quality teaching, and strong ethos with high expectations.

The interviews

All the pupils interviewed were affirming of their schools, and they wanted to 'do well' in their time there. In particular, they liked to feel and be secure in what they were doing and how they were treated, and they liked school as a place where they could meet with their friends. They volunteered compar-isons with other schools where they knew there was criminality and, in their view, it would be dangerous for them to go to such schools. With a few exceptions, the pupils were able to say how well they were doing; to describe the assessment systems that they were working within; and to provide evidence of their current levels of achievement. Year 10 and Year 11 pupils were aware of those who were not achieving, and said that these pupils were in a minority. They attributed underachievement among their peers to their failure to engage with teachers who were trying to support their learning.

The espoused approach of staff was that *all* pupils were at risk of underachieving:

> We do not do something for one group that we are not doing for another. We have got rid of the expectation of underachievement
>
> (Headteacher)

> All children at are risk ... it is important that children feel valued, and not rejected if they make mistakes. We want children to be successful
>
> (Headteacher)

> All are at risk of underachieving here. We do not target pupils as if they are at risk
>
> (Middle manager)

Within these schools, pupils were not grouped as being 'at risk'. The emphasis was more on raising children's aspirations than on preventing underachievement.

For example, pupils said:

> Coming here has been better. At the other school I was 'brushed off', I didn't speak to teachers and they didn't speak to me, they didn't like me ... if I hadn't come to this school I would have been arrested

> There are good teachers here who help you ... they are down to earth, on the same level, not 'stuck up'. I learn more because I can ask them things

> The results are good here, you know how well you are doing from your test results. My work is marked, and the merits are really good, it makes you feel good

> In Year 8 and 9 I got into a lot of trouble. I was lippy to teachers. I have changed and I didn't realize I was changing but my teachers have seen this and have told me. I feel good about it, and I now know how to react to people, and I have a better attitude.

> I am learning a lot and there are a lot of opportunities. I am doing okay, better than I was. My behaviour and attitude have improved and I am doing well now. I go to [name] College and I don't want to lose this. I am doing a GNVQ in construction, and I am involved with others in a building project in Ghana and I am going there for three weeks in August.

On the other hand, teachers said:

> We feel targets rather than be driven by statistics, we constantly challenge and raise aspirations

The staff as a whole are very committed ... there is a real warmth here ... the kids respond to this 'touchy-feely' place ... a culture of feeling safe and secure has been built up

The expectation by staff of pupils is high ... this is self-perpetuating as the children see this in action

The staff and children enjoy coming to school. We don't dread coming to school. We work hard and get tired, but we enjoy being with the children. We look forward to lessons and we make sure we talk with the children

Senior managers said:

What matters is the culture of having a go and believing that this is worthwhile

What makes a difference is that we feel responsible. The children are ours

A whole range of things make a difference, not just one thing. We have tackled it on all fronts: behaviour, learning support, teacher development. We keep children tied into the school

We aim to make the school a place that is valued by all

This inclusive approach is one that has taken time to develop and it has to be constantly worked for, because there are ongoing challenges. As two headteachers remarked:

Discipline is something that we have to keep on top of, we cannot relax

Every day is traumatic in dealing with the particular needs of children

Criticisms were made of external interventions in schools through centralized government reforms that could potentially damage their ways of working. One headteacher described reforms as creating a 'factory system', pointing out that the linearity of learning, as measured by end of key stage tests, does not sit easily with children's lives.

There was a lot of talk about 'ethos' and what it meant to be actively involved in teaching and learning processes. All stressed the importance of high and appropriate expectations: what is required of senior managers in strategically directing and supporting a positive working consensus within school; what is required of middle managers and teachers in their work in classrooms and in participating in school systems; what is required of pupils and parents in taking an active and responsible approach to learning and achievement. This does not mean that everything runs smoothly all of the time, but it does mean that how pupils engage with pupils, teachers engage with teachers and teachers engage with pupils and parents, was based on warmth, support and encouragement. As one headteacher described:

We are strong on discipline, but we are fair and we listen. We don't bear grudges, and we give kids chances. We don't write people off

This approach is embedded and is demonstrated through how children are talked with and about, and how teachers are disposed to act with children. From the adult perspective, children are 'nurtured', 'loved', and from the child perspective they feel 'respected' and 'understood'. As one Year 10 pupil stated:

> This is a good school. Teachers get on with pupils, pupils get on with teachers. They want you to learn and to be successful. If someone is disruptive then they calm you down and don't send you out of the room

This approach is essential to enabling children to achieve in the classroom. As one subject leader stated, while there are discipline problems, teachers work for 'mutual respect', and they generate enthusiasm for learning by enjoying their work as teachers. Nevertheless, pupil concentration over a (typically) 50-minute lesson, and what can be achieved in that time, was an ongoing matter of debate.

The network of relationships between the school, family and wider community was seen as essential to enabling the children to identify with the school. One senior manager described the approach as: 'school is an extension of family life'. This is not about cosiness, for as one headteacher stated, 'we have close relationships with families – we tell them honestly what we think. We have straight and honest conversations'. It is about shaping a secure context in which challenges and risks associated with learning can be responded to. All the schools were interested in developing and sustaining a 'can do' approach to learning, in which no child is written off because of who they are, where they come from or when they arrived in the school. As two subject leaders from different schools stated:

> We don't patronize children, we don't say 'Oh you poor lamb, what a shame'. We know they are disadvantaged and we know we have to be supportive, but we do not allow the staff or children to use this as an excuse. In other schools I have witnessed a patronizing white, middle-class attitude of you can't achieve because your life won't let you

> We don't let their background act as a crutch. We don't pat children on the head for being at risk, or speak down to children. I approach lessons according to whether I would want my own child to be taught like this

What has been developed within children in these schools is the self-belief that they can achieve, and this is the means through which purposeful working environments have been created.

Leadership for achievement

These schools demonstrate that the formal and officially accepted conceptualizations of leadership located in notions of role incumbency and hierarchy are in place, and there is an acceptance of the technologies needed to manage the systems for data collection and analysis and monitoring pupil achievement. Staff talk a lot about the visibility and influence of the head-teacher in relation to school goals and ethos:

> There were problems in this school regarding the expectations of children. The ethos has been changed ... its all down to the head. A number of teachers have stayed here with him because they share the philosophy ... stability is important
>
> (Senior manager)

> [name] is an excellent head ... all are treated as individuals
>
> (Middle manager)

> We have a hands-on head here, who is there for the kids, and she knows who everyone is. She 'feels their collars' and deals with it
>
> (Middle manager)

Teachers and middle managers alike feel that they are cared about and well supported by senior staff, and headteachers also work closely with children: they know them and provide stable, adult role models. One Year 10 pupil stated, 'the headteacher helps me by stopping me from being sent home'. Another said, 'the headteacher helps me, encourages me to do good work, and I get feedback from her'.

Headteachers work with teachers to sustain a focus on teaching and learning and to build systems that support these processes. One school described its 'team' approach where teachers work collaboratively in designing the curriculum, schemes of work and in monitoring achievement. Teachers engage in peer observation of teaching and, through subsequent discussions, develop richer understandings of the possibilities for improvement.

These schools seek to attract and retain good teachers, they have built clusters of staff who have embedded a particular ethos and its supporting frameworks into the schools. Recruitment, selection processes that appoint the right teachers for the school ethos and systems for recognizing potential for development in staff are all regarded as effective. Nevertheless, staffing remains an ongoing challenge in the schools, and one middle manager talked about how hard she had worked to turn around her department, acknowledging that there were issues remaining about staff quality. But her approach is summed up by, 'We need good teachers, and I do not accept second best'. However, the schools are finding it increasingly difficult to fill vacancies or to cover for long/short-term sick leave. Senior managers are working hard to do what one deputy head described as preventing the feeling of 'helplessness' that can come from staffing problems, and they do this by being active, visible and involved in staffing matters.

Another form of leadership seems to be embedded within the practice in these schools and this centres around how the school works as a community to improve learning experiences (Gunter 2001). The emphasis here is more on human interaction than on the lone leader, and on a wider understanding of the purposes of schooling than just measuring what is officially required. A subject leader talked about core values that supported achievement:

We teach mixed ability because we don't want to create a grammar school within the school. I know who everyone is in my classes, who has a statement, who is gifted and talented, and I receive data on pupil progress. We give a lot of informal feedback and give acknowledgement to children because they need this

What seems to be emerging in these schools are glimpses of emancipatory leadership, where leadership is 'not a function of position [but] represents a conjunction of ideas where leadership is shared and transferred between leaders and followers, each only a temporary designation' (Foster 1989: 49). The structural legitimacy of hierarchy is currently masking this aspect of emerging social practice within the schools and will, no doubt, continue to overshadow it. But there is evidence from within these schools that shows that learning through risk-taking is located in shared spaces of security and trust for staff, as well as pupils. Noddings (2003: 249) has argued that teaching exceeds subject knowledge and expertise:

Working with young children, good teachers are keenly aware that they might have devastating effects or uplifting effects on their students. Some of these effects last, or at least are remembered, for a lifetime. This first great good of teaching – responseability and its positive effects – is clearly relational. Teaching is thoroughly relational, and many of its goods are relational: the feeling of safety in a thoughtful teacher's classroom, a growing intellectual enthusiasm in both teacher and student, the challenge and satisfaction shared by both in engaging new material, the awakening sense (for both) that teaching and life are never-ending moral quests.

Perhaps what we are seeing here is that, in some schools at least, leading teachers exceeds the creation of structures and the giving of direction.

While the potential exists for teachers and students to be leaders, 'do' leading and establish learning leadership interactions, the struggle in working for this each day is especially challenging within an urban setting (Gunter 2005). Education professionals work increasingly within a competitive culture where bidding is the route to securing new resources, and where rationing through categorizing and targeting those in most need is counterbalanced by rewarding those who are already most successful. At a time when generic leadership models focus on organizational structures and cultures, teachers might well succumb to followership by adopting the rhetoric of vision and mission, especially if these seem linked to additional resources. However, if practitioners begin with the lives and interests of the children and how the school can provide a secure environment within which all can take risks in pursuit of learning, then leadership is less about the school as an efficient and effective organization, where the focus is on the conditions in which improvement might happen, and instead is about relational social practice.

The discourse within these schools is about negotiating capabilities and creating opportunities for all children to develop their capabilities, where there is interplay between basic, internal and combined capabilities (Nussbaum 1999). At the time of this study this dynamic was, on balance, very productive through a marked disposition to respond to challenges in ways that revealed resilience. When problems occurred pupils, teachers and senior managers, in the main, found ways to handle these and use them as opportunities to enrich learning. Such an approach is necessary but also exhausting, and requires attention both to strategy and to the 'little things' that arise minute by minute from human encounters. The teachers were very aware that what had been created, and was created anew each day, was extraordinarily important for their pupils, but also had a fragility that was under threat from external interventions. Interventions that were about changing the tasks of teachers (through the national curriculum, inspection, performance management, evaluation) rather than being about enabling teachers to build productive pedagogic relationships in their classrooms (Lingard et al. 2003). If children are to face the risks implicit in learning and achievement, then they need stability generated through positive relational encounters. This needs to begin with an understanding of individual student identity, and how this is not necessarily deviant, but is located within the lives of these students and within the communities where they live and grow. Pupils and their parents will resist schools that impose constructed targets and aspirations that they do not share, but they will work with schools that respect diversity (Gunter in press).

Conclusion

By making pupils (and their teachers) the objects rather than subjects of reform, the current modernization of education is being done to people, rather than being worked for with them. The teaching profession has to walk a tightrope of mediation, ensuring that no harm is done to the legitimate ambitions and capabilities of children they teach, while at the same time being publicly accountable for the 'success' of reforms drawn up at a distance from their contexts and practices.

What characterizes urban schooling is how it can become a site for resistance to this hegemony. The six schools in this study show evidence of pupils (and sometimes staff) who come to school having to be convinced that it is a meaningful and productive contribution to their futures. These schools are clearly meeting this basic requirement – an achievement in itself, given the contexts and communities they serve. But, in order to exceed this, staff need the confidence to articulate a model of practice rooted in their students' needs, and reflecting their aspirations and abilities. They need to be able to bridge the gap between local circumstances and national expectations, and to do so in ways that create positive, relevant learning experiences. In such contexts, 'because you need to know it for the test' will never be a sufficient reason to learn.

There is some evidence from the schools of this beginning to take place, though it could only be uncovered by qualitative enquiry, based on participants talking about their work and how they go about it. Teachers are unsettled, often bemused and certainly frustrated by the requirement to deliver externally determined programmes and outcomes, but their commitment remains local in the classroom and staffroom.

This study shows that the potential does exist to work successfully with pupils in the most demanding of contexts. It also suggests that a good starting point for understanding how to do this, is to examine the notions of risk, resilience and capability, and the ways these are negotiated between teacher and pupil in the classroom.

7

MOVING PRACTICE FORWARD AT THE DISTRICT LEVEL

Mel Ainscow, Andy Howes and Dave Tweddle

LEAs in England are accountable to their electorates and to the Secretary of State for maintained schools in their areas. In this sense they can be seen as part of the democratic process by which educational provision is made available for all children and young people within a local area. However, as explained in Chapter 1, national reforms have gradually eroded the power of LEAs. In essence the stated aim has been to delegate greater responsibility to the level of schools in the belief that this will help to foster improvements in standards. This chapter considers the leadership role of LEAs in relationship to the improvement of urban schools. It presents the findings of a three-year study of the work of one LEA that has been applauded for its success in the area of school improvement. The findings illustrate how, by developing new types of relationships with school leaders, LEA staff helped to move practice forward. At the same time, the study reveals how the approaches used led to the marginalization of some groups of learners.

The two most consistently recurring themes of the Labour government's education policy have been concerned with raising standards and promoting inclusion. The challenge for LEAs has been, and continues to be, the pursuit of these twin aims during a period of fundamental reform in the education service.

During this same period, the power of LEAs has been gradually eroded as greater responsibilities have been delegated to the level of individual schools and their governing bodies, and as many of the powers that previously rested with the LEA have been drawn back to central government. In a sense, therefore, 'decentralization' and 'centralization' have been occurring simultaneously. It is within this contradictory policy context that LEAs have been seeking to develop new ways of working.

The work of LEA staff has to be seen in relation to structures and relationships that have been fundamentally reformed over the last few years. These changes reflect moves from what Stoker (2003) calls the 'traditional public administration' approach to service management, towards what he describes as 'new public management'. Based on a critique of existing forms of service provision, Stoker argues that the public management approach involves 'market-like disciplines', including the introduction of a purchaser–provider divide, and the development of performance targets and incentives.

As noted in Chapter 1, in the field of education these changes have been reflected most significantly in the evolving relationships between schools and their LEA. In particular, schools have become much less dependent on their LEAs. At the same time, the relationship between schools has also changed. This arose largely because competition between schools was used as a strategy to drive up standards and reduce the control of the local authority over provision. The question for us, however, is to what extent does this foster equity within the system?

An example of practice

With this question in mind, we examine the work of one apparently successful LEA, looking in particular at how its approach to school improvement relates to government requirements, as laid out in the *Code of Practice on LEA – School Relations* (DfEE 2001). In particular, we consider how far its success reflects the requirements of the *Code* and to what extent its activities are fostering the development of more inclusive schools.

The *Code of Practice on LEA–School Relations* makes explicit the principles, expectations, powers and responsibilities that must guide the work of LEAs in relation to schools. In particular, it lays down the principle that LEA intervention in schools must be 'in inverse proportion to success', and places clear responsibilities on LEAs to intervene in schools found to have serious weaknesses or placed in special measures following an Ofsted inspection.

Our LEA story is set during a period of three years when the national education system was subject to these deep changes in roles and responsibilities. The experiences and struggles of the particular LEA in respect to these changes, therefore, throws light on the impact of these reforms.

During the period 1998–2001 we were privileged to be able to observe closely the work of staff within this local authority as they worked together to engage with the challenges of creating a newly established LEA. The overall aim of our study, which was commissioned by the LEA, was to strengthen its work in supporting school improvement, while at the same time collecting evidence that could inform wider understandings in the field. It focused specifically on the work of a team of school improvement officers (SIOs), but also involved listening to the views of other stakeholders, including, where appropriate, school staff, pupils, parents, officers, governors and elected members.

During the three years of our involvement in the LEA there was increasing evidence that its school improvement strategy was paying off. Test and examination results rose across all phases of the service, with improvement rates in the key stage 2 tests among the highest nationally. And while over the period the LEA had up to 15 schools categorized by Ofsted as either requiring special measures or as having serious weaknesses, by early 2001 the figures were down to just two schools with serious weaknesses. In addition, some schools that had previously been in crisis, subsequently received positive inspection reports. As a result, in its inspection report on the LEA, Ofsted stated, 'This is a remarkable, unique record that is not paralleled elsewhere in the country'.

In order to make sense of what all of this involved we developed a typology of the roles that we saw SIOs taking on. These were as follows:

- *The 'face of the LEA'*: Here the SIO appeared as a figure of authority, standing for the weighty bureaucratic body that is the LEA – very useful in dealing with personnel issues and in reassuring or challenging governors, staff or parents. In this respect we noted many examples of the role taken by SIOs in addressing sensitive personnel issues in schools.
- *The 'sounding board'*: This was where the SIO could be seen as a respected, trusted colleague to whom heads, in particular, could relate the details of a situation and so create an opportunity for consideration out loud of various options for action. In some such situations the SIO seemed to act as a listener/counsellor, a person able to give appropriate attention, especially to a head involved in complex, emotionally demanding situations. Here the SIO could be viewed as a personal support to the head who might otherwise feel quite isolated.
- *The model*: SIOs were sometimes seen as professionals with some breadth of experience in particular areas, who by their practice communicated possible (desirable) ways of achieving certain goals. For example, we were told that some heads tended to ignore the potential of data in forming an understanding of their school, being more naturally inclined to spend their time as a key figure in the school community. So the SIO role would involve working alongside them on such aspects, to realize the potential.
- *The challenger*: This seemed to involve SIOs in taking on the role of questioner, with a brief to push through to greater clarity or commitment on an issue or agenda. In the view of one primary head, the SIO who worked in her school was astute enough to probe through to the reality behind the rhetoric. She explained how in going through plans or records, where previously advisors would have been quite content to listen and go away believing the good news, the SIO would ask questions and probe more. In this particular case, the head invited the SIO to challenge her, to push her in a school in which it would be easy to be complacent.
- *The link*: We found that part of this role depended on the quality of teamwork between SIOs, as heads perceived it. Sometimes the role of link became that of providing a postal service, dropping things off to schools. Often SIOs seemed to simply drop in and out of schools in this way, keeping a certain low level of contact which might be useful in all sorts of ways, not least in picking up incidental information about what was happening. Indeed it struck us that providing a postal service might be a kind of excuse.
- *Supporter*: Here we saw the SIO as a person taking the side of the school/ headteacher in practical ways against external threats. With regard to

Ofsted inspections, in particular, the SIO sometimes took a role in the preparation period. There was no doubt that this was appreciated by many of the heads.

• *Interested friend*: Several times the SIO was mentioned as someone who would come to events such as concerts or presentations, and be informally involved in the life of the school as community. Always heads associated this with building relationships with staff.

Social learning

As we have seen, the approach to school improvement developed within the LEA involved a complex set of interconnected strategies, implemented by a team of hard-working and committed SIOs. In this sense, much can be learnt from what they did and how they did it. Having said that, our close involvement led us to believe that a deeper analysis was needed in order to understand the full significance of what had occurred over the three year period. Such an analysis also has implications for conceptualizing the forms of learning that can occur as a result of engaging with the LEA's story.

It is sometimes argued that school improvement is technically simple but socially complex. In many ways this applies to this account. These is no doubt that staff within the LEA were remarkably creative in inventing ways of working that stimulated and supporting change within schools. However, we remain unconvinced that simply teaching new people how to use these approaches, or, indeed, lifting the approaches in order to reproduce them in a different context, would have the powerful impact that they clearly had within the particular LEA. The problem with such an approach is that it overlooks the social processes of learning that enabled the strategies to have their powerful impact. Consequently, we reflected further on our evidence in order to seek a deeper understanding of what was involved in these 'social processes of learning'.

Wenger (1998) provides a framework that can be used to analyse learning in social contexts. At the centre of this framework is the concept of a community of practice, a social group engaged in the sustained pursuit of a shared enterprise. This suggests that practices are ways of negotiating meaning through social action. Wenger argues that learning within a given community can often be best explained within the intertwining of reification and participation. He suggests that these are complementary processes, in that each has the capacity to repair the ambiguity of meaning the other can engender. So, for example, we observed how particular strategies would be developed as part of SIO planning activities and summarized in a set of guidance for action, providing a codified reification of intended practice. However, the meaning and practical implications of these strategies only became clear as they were tried in the field and discussed between colleagues. In this way, participation resulted in social learning that could not be produced solely by reification alone. At the same time, the reified products, such as the policy documents that emerged, served as a kind of memory of practice, cementing in place the new learning.

We can, then, use the notion of communities of practice to offer some further explanation of what happened in the LEA. It does seem that the key to the LEA's success lay in its success in encouraging networking at different levels within the service. In particular, the links encouraged between head-teachers seemed to encourage the creation of many different communities of practice that helped to break down the sense of intellectual and, indeed, emotional isolation that had characterized their previous working lives. Then, through a complex set of strategies and processes, the LEA facilitated parti-cipation and reification procedures that helped such learning communities to grow.

Such an analysis seems to provide a way of describing the processes that were at the heart of the authority's success. So, to what extent is this con-sistent with what the government has in mind for the future of LEAs?

Analysing the experience

While the LEA in this study was established before the actual publication of the *Code of Practice*, it was clearly designed with similar principles in mind. When we look more closely, however, some important differences of emphasis become apparent. These differences seem to relate directly to the social processes of learning that contributed to the ways in which practices developed within the LEA.

An analysis of the *Code of Practice* document points to certain key areas of responsibility that LEAs are expected to take on. In particular, LEAs are expected to monitor the performance of their schools in order to 'support and challenge them where necessary.' The *Code* suggests that monitoring of schools should be based on 'routinely available information' such as test data, Ofsted reports and information from school–self review. Indeed, it concludes that an 'Authority which makes effective use of the full range of information which is routinely available to it will rarely need to visit schools solely for the purpose of gathering further information' (DfEE 2001). Certainly, the SIOs in our study saw themselves as supporting and, where necessary, challenging school led improvement strategies. However, all of this was set within a wider context of relationships and procedures that meant that they had developed a deep knowledge of what went on in the schools. In this way they were able to engage senior school staff in detailed discussion of improvement strategies, bringing to bear their detailed knowledge of particular people (staff and pupils), contexts, policies and practices. It is difficult to see how such understandings could be achieved simply through the use of 'routinely available information' of the sort outlined within the *Code*. SIOs felt that they knew their schools, and that it was this knowledge which made their inter-ventions authentic. By and large, headteachers were in agreement.

The SIOs in our study became increasingly competent at analysing the annual package of performance data provided for schools while also having detailed knowledge of the strengths and weaknesses of practice within each school. This meant that they were in a good position to comment on a school's proposed targets, coming from an informed yet different position from that of the headteacher. In addition, the LEA produced a 'profile' for each school, a very useful digest for comparison of results.

During the run-in to a school's inspection, SIOs tended to want to help schools to present themselves in the most favourable way. So, for example, it might be suggested to a headteacher who had disappointing test results in relation to the school's targets that more children could be placed on the special education needs register. This implied that greater progress could not have been expected from these particular pupils. Similarly, a headteacher might be helped to develop a 'script' as to what should be said in the written self-review documents that are prepared for the inspection team, focusing on areas of evidence that seemed to be potentially problematic. Here specific attention would be paid to the importance of terminology. So, for example, one SIO said to a head that it was important to avoid words such as 'sustaining' or 'consolidating', which might imply an element of coasting. On the other hand, a phrase such as 'striving to improve' might be a sensible comment when addressing areas of what seem to be statistical weakness.

In relation to such processes we were left reflecting upon about their intentions. Was the purpose of analysing pupil performance data intended to inform school improvement activity, or, in cases like this, was it simply a form of 'window dressing' in preparation for the visit of Ofsted inspectors? At the same time, did these processes encourage school staff to marginalize some groups of pupils? If so, we concluded, there must be a real danger that the emphasis on short-term targets and strategies could act as a barrier to longer term, sustainable development in respect to the learning of all pupils within a school.

The *Code of Practice* places enormous emphasis on the LEA's duty to identify and support schools causing concern. Here it stresses that the prime focus should be to ensure that 'an effective headteacher and senior management team are in place, working with an effective governing body in pursuit of a good and deliverable action plan'. Our observations indicated that it was through their increasingly close knowledge of the schools that SIOs were able to pick up signs that things were not altogether well. In some instances schools were then placed on the LEA's list of schools causing concern. This also signalled that a more formal support strategy was to be involved, with the headteacher, chair of governors and link SIO meeting with a senior LEA officer termly in order to ensure that appropriate measures were in place. As a result, it was possible to mobilize additional human resources in order to enable a school to address a growing difficulty.

Actions such as these often seemed to be effective, not least in preventing a school from getting into difficulty with Ofsted. However, we found that increasingly SIOs began to question the long-term effects of this approach, raising the question of what happens after the LEA has been successful in preventing a school from being categorized as 'special measures' or 'serious weakness'. Their worry was that having helped a school to 'patch up', this might provide it with the excuse for not taking serious action to address its difficulties. In this context, of course, the LEA's commitment to be seen to have fewer schools in difficulties (particularly in the run-in to a forthcoming LEA inspection), had the potential to create yet further barriers to school improvement.

Standards and inclusion

Phillips and Harper-Jones (2003) claim that 'New' Labour's education policy has been characterized by four themes: 'a determination to raise educational standards; a quest to undertake the modernisation of educational systems, structures and practices; a commitment to choice and diversity within education; and a preoccupation with ... the culture of performativity'. These themes are, of course, in many ways a continuation of the marketizing and centralizing policies of previous Conservative governments and are what have led some American researchers to describe England as 'a laboratory where the effects of market-like mechanisms are more clearly visible' (Finkelstein and Grubb 2000). However, what possibly differentiated this Labour government from its predecessor was a 'fifth theme', which Phillips and Harper-Jones rather gloss over. That is, a broad commitment to equity in and through education, variously badged as 'inclusion' or 'social inclusion'.

This is arguably the most troubling aspect of the study we have summarized in this chapter. As we have explained, it revealed how attempts to move from a dependent relationship between LEAs and their schools, towards one that places greater emphasis on independence are socially complex. However, it also showed how, within a context that values aggregated test and examination scores and the outcomes of inspection as the criteria for determining success, such moves can act as a barrier to the development of a more inclusive education system.

Towards the end of our study, we interviewed an external consultant who had assisted the LEA in its preparations for the Ofsted inspection, looking specifically at its approach to pupils categorized as having special educational needs, and other vulnerable groups. He suggested that salaries within the LEA were evidence of what he saw as 'a pecking order' of officers, influencing the way priorities were signalled within the service. SIOs, he said, were the best paid people in the department. He went on to describe the difficulties faced by lower status staff, such as educational psychologists or advisory teachers, going into a school to help make some inclusive arrangement for an individual child experiencing difficulties and seen to be pulling in the opposite direction to the SIO.

The consultant told of how, with an Ofsted inspection looming, some SIOs had 'helped youngsters out of the window' so that classes would become easier to manage. The SIO brief, as he understood it, was to get schools out of special measures very quickly, or to prevent them from going into special measures in the first place. He explained:

> They have done it really well. However, my argument is, in doing that, what they are actually doing is not promoting inclusion. They are in many ways working to the opposite direction, which has resulted in children being excluded, sometimes in groups. It has also resulted in students being removed to special schools for a term, without a statement, just to see how he gets on and say no more ... They don't go back. Once they are out, they stay out. That is a long, long way removed from saying that your responsibility is to provide an education for all the children that are in your community.

We collected evidence of other similar experiences. We also noted how, more generally, deficit thinking appeared to influence the expectations in some schools of certain groups of learners who were seen as 'lacking something' (Trent et al. 1998). It was also evident that there was a strong expectation across the LEA that pupils with certain types of characteristics had to be educated in contexts away from the mainstream classroom. All of this led us to conclude that the apparently successful efforts of this particular LEA to respond to the government's demands for improved standards had, in practice, created barriers to the participation of certain groups of pupils within its schools.

Some implications

During the final year of the study, we were able to stimulate discussion among LEA staff as to how they might place more emphasis on making the LEA's school improvement strategy more inclusive. In raising this issue we argued that the current context offered a range of opportunities. On the other hand, we explained how certain contradictions in national policy tended to act as barriers to progress.

Looking first at the opportunities, we noted how a number of recent government initiatives had encouraged those within the education system to address issues that are relevant to the development of inclusive practices. For example, the 2000 reforms in the National Curriculum had emphasized the principle of inclusion; the national literacy and numeracy strategies had stimulated debate and, to some degree, experimentation in classroom practice; and organizational processes associated with Education Action Zones and Excellence in Cities were encouraging greater cooperation between schools. Meanwhile, a recent Ofsted document had offered a new definition of what was meant by an effective school when it stated: 'An educationally inclusive school is one in which the teaching and learning, achievements, attitudes and well being of every young person matters. Effective schools are educationally inclusive schools' (Ofsted 2000).

However, despite these hopeful signs, we were conscious that many practitioners felt that the government's plethora of reforms has tended to encourage fragmentation in the field, as schools and LEAs were required to collude with procedures that offered additional finance for projects that were often disconnected from one another and short-term in their aspirations. In these ways, strategies intended to foster the government's twin agendas of 'raising standards' and 'promoting inclusion' seemed to be pulling them in opposite directions.

We invited the LEA staff to consider how they might move forward in ways that would bring together the so-called 'standards' and 'inclusion' agendas. In so doing, we argued that the LEA would need to have a strong strategy for change in order for it to be successful in addressing this complex set of issues. Research on educational innovations indicates the importance of personal meaning (e.g. Fullan 1991). Put simply, change requires learning, and successful change involves stakeholders in developing a deeper understanding of the purposes of a particular innovation and how these relate to existing practices. Logic suggests, then, that the more complex the change, the more learning that is required.

Changing cultures

The analysis presented in this chapter confirms that LEAs can have a significant role to play in respect of processes of school improvement. However, it also indicates that attempts by LEAs to move schools in a more inclusive direction within the current overall policy context are likely to be problematic to say the least. In particular, we have to remember that much of what goes on within organizations, such as LEAs and schools, is largely taken for granted and therefore rarely discussed. In other words, practices are manifestations of organizational cultures (Schein 1985; Angelides and Ainscow 2000). This leads us to assume that many of the barriers experienced by learners arise from existing ways of thinking. Consequently, strategies for developing inclusive practices have to involve interruptions to thinking in order to encourage 'insiders' to explore overlooked possibilities for moving practice forward (Ainscow 2003a).

It seems to us, therefore, that significant progress requires an engagement with questions of purpose at all levels of the education system. Such an engagement could, perhaps, be facilitated by the adoption of Stoker's notion of public value management, with its emphasis on network governance. This would suggest that the way forward is for LEAs to engage their communities of practice in a process of debate about what is meant by quality and achievement in education in a way that emphasizes equity and social justice. It would also imply the negotiation of new, interdependent relationships between schools, LEAs and their wider communities.

Introducing such an approach in the current context, with its cocktail of competing agendas and confusion about forms of governance, is, however, far from straightforward. We recall, for example, a meeting in one particular LEA that had been called to discuss a proposal to establish networks of schools. Eventually, one secondary headteacher, while acknowledging that he had enjoyed the debate, commented, 'OK, but, what's in this for me and my school?' He went on to argue that the idea of collaboration would only 'take off' if the key stakeholders could see that there would be significant, practical benefits for their own school or organization. In other words, he would need to be convinced that the proposed arrangement would enable his school to move forward.

All of this seems to suggest that self-interest is, in practice, a predictable and important component of interdependency. Johnson and Johnson (1994), for example, suggest that individuals become interdependent when 'an event that affects one member affects them all'. This means that participants need first to understand and then to experience the tangible benefits of interdependent working arrangements.

We argue, then, that levers need to be found that will be powerful in encouraging the development of interdependence while, at the same time, easing those involved in a more inclusive direction. Through our own work, we have tried to 'map' factors at the LEA level that have the potential to either facilitate or inhibit the promotion of inclusive practices in schools. These are all factors which education departments either control directly or over which they can at least exert considerable influence (Ainscow and Tweddle 2003). Our research suggests that two factors, particularly when they are closely linked, seem to be superordinate to all others. These are *clarity of purpose* and the *forms of evidence* that are used to measure educational performance.

Within the field there is still considerable confusion about what 'inclusion' actually means (Ainscow et al. 2000). To some extent, this lack of clarity might be tracked back to central government policy statements. On the other hand, our experience has been that a well-orchestrated debate about definition can have leverage with respect to fostering the conditions within which schools can feel encouraged to move in a more inclusive direction. Such a debate needs to involve all stakeholders within a local community, including politicians and indeed the media. It must also involve those within the local education department so that they have clarity as to what must drive their actions.

Our search for 'levers' has also led us to acknowledge the importance of evidence. In essence it leads us to conclude that, within education systems, 'what gets measured gets done'. So, for example, LEAs are required to collect far more statistical data than ever before. This is widely recognized as a double-edged sword precisely because it is such a potent lever for change. On the one hand, data are required in order to monitor the progress of children, evaluate the impact of interventions, review the effectiveness of policies and processes, plan new initiatives and so on. In these senses, data can, justifiably, be seen as the life-blood of continuous improvement. However, if effectiveness is evaluated on the basis of narrow, even inappropriate, performance indicators, then the impact can be deeply damaging. While appearing to promote the causes of accountability and transparency, the use of data can in practice conceal more than it reveals, invite misinterpretation and, worst of all as we have illustrated in this paper, have a perverse effect on the behaviour of professionals. This has led the current 'audit culture' to be described as a 'tyranny of transparency' (Strathern 2000).

All of this suggests that great care needs to be exercised in deciding what evidence is collected and, indeed, how it is used. English LEAs are required by government to collect particular data. Given national policies, they cannot opt out of collecting such data on the grounds that their publication might be misinterpreted, or that they may influence practice in an unhelpful way. On the other hand, LEAs are free to collect additional evidence that can then be used to evaluate the effectiveness of their own policy and practice with respect to progress towards greater inclusion. The challenge for LEAs is, therefore, to harness the potential of evidence as a lever for change while avoiding the problems described earlier. Our own work suggests that the starting point for making decisions about the evidence to collect should be with an agreed definition of inclusion. In other words, we must 'measure what we value' rather than, as is often the case, 'valuing what we can measure'.

Our central argument, then, is that the challenges of strategic management at the LEA level have changed as the policy context has changed. We believe that the development and management of interdependent working relationships may be the means by which LEAs can work more effectively with their schools in improving the quality of education for all children and young people.

8

SUPPORTING SCHOOLS IN DIFFICULT CIRCUMSTANCES: THE ROLE OF SCHOOL TO SCHOOL COOPERATION

Mel Ainscow, Mel West and Maria Nicolaidou

The previous chapter concluded that the way to improve the quality of education for all children and young people is through the development of interdependent working relationships. In this way better use can be made of expertise within schools to develop more effective practices. This chapter explores how this might be achieved by describing and analysing how three relatively successful schools partnered a school that was in difficulty in order to foster improvements in its work. The analysis concludes that school to school cooperation offers greater possibilities for school improvement than existing strategies that rely solely on the efforts of individual headteachers who are expected to act as 'hero innovators'. At the same time, it argues that the introduction of such approaches is far from easy. Consequently, considerable care needs to be taken in introducing such approaches more widely.

The government has made various attempts to improve schools that are seen to be a cause for concern. One approach that was introduced was that of the Fresh Start initiative. Modelled on ideas imported from the USA, this approach placed particular emphasis on the role of the headteacher as the key, leading to the use in the media of the term 'superhead'.

In England Fresh Start was presented as 'an option' for local education authorities to use in tackling school failure. Blackstone (2000) argued that it offered a 'radical approach to securing school improvement for failing schools showing insufficient evidence of recovery'. The scheme under which the worst performing schools, as identified by Ofsted, are relaunched under a new name, with a new headteacher, without staff who had been unsuccessful in reapplying for their old jobs and with extra cash has, however, been dogged by controversy, with the resignation of the first four 'superheads' to be appointed.

This chapter documents a rather different approach. It tells the story of an urban highschool that serves one of the country's most economically deprived areas. The school was fifteenth from the bottom of the national

GCSE league table when the former Education Secretary, David Blunkett, announced a crackdown on poor examination results in March 2000. All schools where less than 15 percent of students achieved five A* to C grades in GCSEs for three consecutive years would be given a 'Fresh Start'. At this particular school, the relevant figure that year was just 7 percent.

Working together

In fact, the school did not close. Instead, three relatively successful schools in the same LEA partnered it in order to foster improvements in the school's work. Cooperation between the headteachers of the four schools was the central strategy used. The LEA provided support for the initiative and some additional funding was provided by the Standards and Effectiveness Unit at the DfES. We were asked by the heads of the schools involved to evaluate the project.

There were approximately 450 students on the roll, although the school was originally intended for 1000. As we have explained, it serves one of the most deprived areas in the country and had examination results that might have warranted a 'Fresh Start'. However, an alternative solution was suggested by the headteacher of another local high school. His initial proposal was that he should be placed in charge of both schools. However, since the existing head of the school in difficulty was due to retire, the LEA had already advertised for a successor. In the event, the idea of having a team of head-teachers was agreed. This suggestion was much more acceptable to the gov-erning body, the members of which were committed to the employment of a headteacher for their school.

The actual mix of expertise provided by the consultant heads proved to be very important. In particular, one had a strong track record in relation to finances and resources; another had a reputation for target setting and put-ting in place strategies enabling students to work towards individual learning targets; and a third had expertise in marketing and working with unions. As we will explain, when the story unfolded it became clear that these were exactly the kinds of area that outsiders could address, leaving those within the school to concentrate on leadership and capacity-building.

By the time of the interviews for a new headteacher in April 2000, the basis for the partnership arrangement was largely in place. Nevertheless, the suc-cessful candidate was given the choice as to whether or not she actually wanted to work with the proposed consultancy team. In that sense, therefore, the decision to go ahead was ultimately hers.

From Easter to the end of the summer term 2000, the three heads worked with the headteacher-elect to produce a 'comprehensive plan for raising achievement'. They also agreed that their roles would be mainly as con-sultants, each contributing the equivalent of one day a week of support and advice. From the outset it was noted that the new head and the school's governing body would always 'have the last word'. This meant that as she talked with her new colleagues it was absolutely clear to them that she was 'in charge' of the school.

The work of the consultant headteachers

Once the project was announced to the staff there were some signs of mistrust and resentment towards what was proposed and how it was going to be put in place. The fact that some of the staff had to take early retirement or reapply for their jobs caused particular turbulence, and some of the teachers remember the period as being a 'confusing and stressing time'.

Apparently, the proposed redundancies overshadowed the events surrounding the retirement of the existing headteacher. Some staff stated that they could be supportive of the in-coming head because they felt that the changes that she and the consulting heads were proposing made sense, especially those related to the curriculum. At the same time, others recall having doubts and uncertainties about what was being proposed.

This period of mixed reactions presented the three consultant heads with a series of dilemmas and sensitive situations as they explored ways of developing their new roles. Initially, the retiring head was still in position and this made it difficult for them to collect further information and intervene directly. They were also conscious that some of the staff might react negatively to their presence in the school since there were understandable loyalties to the retiring headteacher.

Once the heads did begin visiting the school, however, they became increasingly concerned about what they found. For example one of them explained:

> The shock was that the finances were in a very poor state and the school was vastly overstaffed. In fact, it was uneconomic. The staff had a perception that it was all ok … They had dug themselves little holes and jumped in with tin hats on. They had low expectations not only of themselves but also of the students and it didn't take us long to find that out. We didn't find anything that was unexpected other than some comments like, 'what do you expect from children like these'.

The team asked staff to tell them what was wrong. Recalling some of the responses, one of the visiting heads commented:

> We felt that the more we talked to them, the more we actually got the truth. There were lots of things: staff living in the past; others saying, plod on with your head down and get paid; some saying, staff do very little; others feeling neglected, saying they had received no training. They had a middle school mentality: lack of leadership; staff too friendly and relaxed; no monitoring; frustration and a feeling that it was not going anywhere, therefore they felt it wasn't worthwhile. There was a culture of underachievement. There was no culture of children working after school; a lack of determination; no vision; lack of challenge; no rigour; no will; no cooperation; no consistency; and no back-up from senior staff.

One head remembered how, during a staff meeting, the three consultants presented their views on a series of overhead projector slides. This including an analysis of the school's targets for improvement: what had been achieved and what might have been achieved. He recalled that some members of staff were clearly shocked. He also said that he 'went through *their* perceptions of the place, which also shocked and somehow angered them. The point was that it was in fact their perception of what went on'.

Referring to the same staff meeting, one of the other consultant heads said that this was probably the most significant moment in the whole initiative. The consultant head who made the presentation explained:

> I took all the value-added data for the LEA and I put a table up which showed the 21 high schools (it hadn't any names on it) and it went from best to worse and I asked where they thought they were as a school. And they all thought they were in the middle or, possibly, even to the left of the middle. And, when I told them they were significantly 21st out of 21, they were absolutely shocked. They wouldn't believe it. But the previous Ofsted report hadn't done them any favours because it seemed to be saying that they were doing the best but kids didn't want to go to school. It [the Ofsted report] concentrated on the challenging circumstances without actually looking at the challenges. That was a very interesting moment. Once I had done that ... at that point I think they were prepared to move on.

A new headteacher

Once the new headteacher was appointed she took every available opportunity to let the staff know that she was, to use her own words, 'the person in charge ... It was my school and not the other three heads'. Recalling that period, one senior member of staff commented:

> She showed a lot of drive and determination to make things happen. She wanted the kids bringing in equipment in school. Basically, running the school like her place, like a normal school. No-one was arguing about that.

On the other hand, the announcement in the autumn of 2000 that there was to be a programme of staff redundancies had a marked impact on staff morale. Many staff remembered this as a very difficult time, particularly for those colleagues who had been at the school for many years. Some staff had to reapply for and be interviewed for their jobs.

During the early part of the 2000–01 school year the three consultant heads carried out observations around the school and interviewed members of the staff, asking for their perceptions of their school. However, some staff recalled that they did not have a personal interview with the new head, as they had been promised. Some felt that this was something that was overlooked. Others were unconvinced by the way in which they were interviewed, arguing, as one person put it, that they felt that they were all 'tarred with the same brush'.

In telling the story, the headteacher of the school focused mainly on her own activities, with only occasional mention of the work of the three consultants. Specifically, she felt that they had made a major contribution in helping her to restructure the staffing. She also referred to the fact that there was a phase when things were really difficult and so one of the heads would ring her each evening, at the end of the school day. She recalled that this form of personal support was, for her, particularly significant. At the same time, she was firm in her view that 'turning the school round' could not have happened without her presence and leadership from within.

Her account says much about her personal management strategy. In particular, she remembers being struck initially by the low expectations that were held in the school. For example, she noticed that very few of the children brought bags to school, in which they could carry books and equipment. She decided that she must insist that every student had a bag. She recalled what happened:

> So, I did this sort of big speech of how it all starts from here. You know, head up, shoulders back, in we go. And I just said, you've all got to bring bags and if you haven't got a bag tomorrow you will be sent to my office. If they hadn't got a bag I gave them an Aldi carrier bag. I said, I want you to give that back tomorrow. And bingo, by the end of the first week every child had a bag.

She recalls that many of the teachers said it would not be possible to implement such a requirement, but she persisted and the strategy was successful. She saw this as being a key factor in getting students to do their homework, since without bags there was little transfer of books between home and school.

Similarly, she persisted in implementing policies about the completion of homework, the wearing of school uniform, lunchtime arrangements and on the raising of school attendance rates. In the case of this latter policy, she established a team of people who chase up students who are not attending.

Patrolling the school

One example of the new head's leadership style could be seen in the introduction of 'school patrols'. The senior management team of four developed a model of working whereby each of them patrols the school, going in and out of every classroom a number of times during each day. The head also encouraged all of them to follow a similar style of intervention to the one that she modelled, a style that is insistent on certain kinds of behaviour and attitude.

Shadowing the head on these patrols was an interesting experience. She walks directly into every classroom and, without being invited to do so, speaks across the teacher, addressing students and, at the same time, addressing the member of staff as well. She explains that she is conscious of appearing to undermine her colleagues, and this is clearly a potential danger. On the other hand she believes that the way she does this appears to avoid this trap.

Often, during a classroom visit, she will speak to an individual student whom she is 'checking on'. Where students are reported to her by a teacher as misbehaving, or not doing their work appropriately, she then talks directly to them. For example, in one classroom, in a rather exaggerated tone of voice, she addressed one of the students, saying: 'I'm very disappointed with you, Darren, and I want to apologise to Miss. She comes here to teach and she certainly does not have to tolerate such behaviour'. In these situations her manner is both supportive of her colleagues and, at the same time, critical of certain student's actions, many of whom are clearly intimidated by the experience.

At times she can appear to be quite aggressive with individual students, particularly those who are found to be standing outside the room, having been sent out of class by a teacher. Similarly, students seen to be misbehaving between lessons or not getting to their next class quickly, may be withdrawn and given the task of collecting litter around the school. In such ways, it seemed that the head and her senior team appear to take personal responsibility for inappropriate behaviour. They also use similar strategies for celebrating the efforts and achievements of students.

In discussing this style of 'management by walking about', the head explained that it is extremely demanding of her time and, indeed, the time of her senior colleagues. It also means that she takes on a lot of the discipline issues that arise within the school. Nevertheless, it appeared to have been a highly successful strategy for supporting staff and, indeed, transforming the overall climate within the school. The head summed this up:

> The kids expect me to be in evidence. And my leadership team do the same. And that's why it's a very well-disciplined school now. You walk around now and what you will see is an extraordinary level of kids on time for lessons.

Subsequently, the head took the decision to reduce the use of this strategy in order that she could have what she describes as 'a more balanced set of relationships' with the students in the school.

Determining the impact

During this time, considerable changes were made in the curriculum, particularly at Year 10 where new vocational programmes were introduced. Cooperation between the partner schools gradually involved other groups of staff, not least in order to address difficulties in certain subject areas. Attention was also given to the improvement of the physical environment, through decoration and displays, and there were further plans for improving those parts of the school that were rather unpleasant.

Two years into the work of the partnership, HMI argued that there was evidence of a 'massive change' in the school's ethos, with teaching and behaviour, in particular, improving significantly. The proportion of students gaining five higher GCSEs rose to 10 percent in 2001, truancy levels had been halved and the proportion of pupils gaining five or more A to G grades improved by 20 percentage points to 94 percent. Then, in the summer of

2003, more striking improvements were announced, with 33 percent of students achieving at least five grade A* to C at GCSE.

The head herself felt that the partnership arrangement was beneficial when advertising for new members of staff, particularly in a context where people tended to be reluctant to take the risk of moving to schools that are in difficulty. For example:

> We actually interviewed somebody who was a front-runner for the secondary science post in the summer and he said at the end of the interview, if this project all falls apart this school could close, couldn't it? We said yes, but it won't!

The three consultant heads argued that the whole experience had been a steep learning curve for them, too and, indeed, for all the staff that had been involved. They also pointed out that the project involved an element of risk-taking, since if it had failed 'the consultant heads had quite a lot to lose, as well as the school'.

As things turned out, the three heads all felt that their involvement has benefited them and their schools. For example, one of them, having been in post for many years during which time his school had become very successful, was convinced that it had helped him to 'think again' about his own practices. He described, too, how discussions with his colleague heads had led him to reflect on different leadership styles.

The same head emphasized the importance of the trust that existed between the three consultants. He reflected that the experience had not been threatening to them since they had a shared goal and shared responsibility: they all wanted the school to succeed. Consequently, they were able to work collaboratively. He was also convinced that the power of the strategy came about as a result of this collaborative emphasis between a group of practising heads:

> The consultant head model can work because it takes some of your time but not all of it, and because we work as a team ... and no matter what you do, money, resources, policy, you can only get schools out of difficulty through positive leadership. I'm convinced of that.

Making sense of the experience

It seems, then, that school to school cooperation *can* be an effective strategy for supporting schools facing difficulties and, indeed, for induction to headship in difficult circumstances. Having said that, we are anxious to stress that it does not present a simple, straightforward recipe that can be lifted and easily replicated in other contexts.

In drawing lessons, therefore, we aspire to provide a commentary that will be useful to others who are interested in moving practice forward in contexts facing similar challenges. However, in doing so we are keen to respect the complexity of what has occurred and, indeed, the limitations of our own investigations.

As we have shown, this particular initiative involved a complex mix of social processes that has clearly had a significant impact on attitudes, relationships, practices and learning outcomes for staff and students alike. It is impossible to say which of the many ingredients has been most significant. This being the case, it seems sensible to assume that it is through the interaction of the different elements that the power of the approach is achieved.

In attempting to make sense of the experience, we draw particular attention to three interconnected strands of activity that would need to be considered by those wishing to adopt a similar approach elsewhere. These strands are preparing the ground, getting together the correct mix of expertise and ensuring trust.

It is clear that the lead-in period was both significant and messy. The period was also rich in events that had the potential to create tensions and even conflict, both in the school and in the wider context. The leadership provided by one of the consultant headteachers who clearly had considerable status and credibility in the district, and his cooperation with senior staff in the LEA were, therefore, essential elements in setting up appropriate arrangements for taking the initiative forward.

Beyond leadership and cooperation, however, there was also a need for considerable skills in diplomacy in negotiating with governors (in the four schools), and in reassuring members of staff who were understandably disturbed by what must have seemed baffling circumstances and unprecedented proposals. Here, loyalties towards the previous regime and policies, and fears about personal career uncertainties, added to the sense of turbulence that existed. And, of course, during the planning phase of the project, those coming in from outside had to deal with the continued presence of the retiring head, who by all accounts was well-respected and admired.

Those who set up the partnership arrangements were, to a large degree, successful in dealing with all these potential difficulties. Consequently, important tasks were carried out prior to the arrival of the newly appointed headteacher, including the formulation of a plan of action based on sound evidence as to the situation on the ground. The availability of such a plan enabled the new head to 'hit the ground running', to an extent that would have been impossible under normal conditions. As a result, she knew what she had to do and she set about her tasks immediately on her arrival at the school.

The decision to involve a team of headteacher consultants, and therefore a group of schools, proved to be an essential factor in the success of the partnership. All the schools were known to be performing well and all three consultant heads were recognized as successful school leaders. But perhaps even more important was the range and types of expertise that together they brought to the situation. In essence they were able to share responsibility for those tasks that have the potential to occupy the time and energy of any newly appointed head, thus leaving this head relatively free to concentrate on those day to day issues that can only be addressed by those who are always available in the school.

As we saw, the areas on which the consultant heads concentrated included external relations and marketing, budgets and resources, staffing and target-setting. Time was also saved in addressing these areas because, unlike the newly appointed head, the three consultants had close knowledge of local arrangements, organizations and people. Meanwhile, the head and her senior team were able to focus most of their energy on the key areas of building supportive relationships and raising expectations. This was achieved by ensuring that they had a much higher level of presence around the school and in the classrooms than is usually the case when new heads and management teams take up their duties.

Their strategies for raising expectations focused on three groups. First, the interventions of the management team encouraged a greater sense of self-esteem among *students*. New policies were introduced, such as those to do with attendance, behaviour and homework, and then, most significantly, persistent and insistent measures were taken to ensure that these policies were consistently implemented throughout the school.

Second, considerable efforts were made to raise expectations among the *staff*. In particular, attention was given to ensuring that all staff members felt that they always had support available as they dealt with difficulties in their lessons and around the school. And, where necessary, in-service training was provided to support them in responding to new requirements. All of this was carried out within what can only be described as an 'upbeat' atmosphere, where success was constantly recognized and celebrated. Finally, the head-teacher paid attention to convincing the *local community* that the school was changing, and to convincing parents that it could achieve good results for their children.

While having an appropriate range of expertise was a necessary condition for the success of the partnership, in itself it was insufficient. Also needed were attitudes and relationships within which all this expertise could be used in an effective way. It is here that the potential for difficulty becomes so obvious.

First of all, there is the potential for difficulties created by factors at the macro-policy level. In particular, within a context in which national educational policies are based on the principles of parental choice and competition between schools, what are the incentives for headteachers to offer one another help and support? And, within such a context, how can arrangements be made that will allow open and trusting working patterns to be established?

Then, at the micro-level, there is a relative minefield of potential difficulties when a team of established and successful headteachers appear to have superordinate status over a newly appointed and inexperienced head. This relationship also had a gender dimension, with three established male heads supporting a novice female head. The evidence is that those involved managed to avoid these possible difficulties, and their approach is worthy of close scrutiny by those in other contexts who are seeking to follow a similar trail. Once again here, we stress that the account does not provide a recipe but, rather, a basis for reviewing necessary ingredients.

An important factor was the strong and open relationships that existed between the three consultant heads who knew each other prior to the initiative. They then spent considerable time in helping one another to clarify their roles, including the need to define the boundaries of their activities. In addition, protocols were devised that meant that each partner was certain as to what was to be expected and how difficulties would be addressed.

The establishment of clarity on roles, responsibilities and responses between the three consultants was, then, the basis of agreements with the new head. Perhaps as a result, she was able to define her own boundaries of activity in respect of what the outsiders would be seeking to contribute. And, as we have seen, she was very firm and determined in confirming to everybody involved that it was 'her school' and that it was her responsibility to 'turn it round'.

Implications

At this point it is important to remind readers of the limitations of our study, some of which suggest certain reservations that need to be kept in mind. We are aware that, despite the care that we have taken to check the accuracy of our evidence, we can only provide a partial account of everything that has happened. There are also issues arising from the relatively short timescale of our investigations. So, for example, while we have pointed to evidence of striking progress in three years or so, we cannot give any informed judgement as to the potential for longer term growth.

Here, of course, as with all forms of school improvement, the issue of sustainability remains a challenge. In this respect there are a number of factors that are rather particular to the context we have described. First, the school is in an environment where families have a choice of schools within easy distance. This being the case, there remains the worry that however much progress the school makes with respect to the quality of education it provides, other local schools with stronger reputations will continue to be the preferred choice. If so, the school will inevitably experience a range of constraints that will set limits on how much further improvement can be achieved, particularly with respect to the improvement of aggregate test and examination scores.

Second, there are uncertainties as to the capacity of the existing arrangements to support longer term improvement efforts. In particular, we do not know whether the fact that outsiders have taken responsibility for a range of key strategic issues has allowed those within the school to develop their own expertise in addressing these areas. Could it be, for example, that allowing a new headteacher to concentrate most of her efforts on certain tasks means that she has missed out on other professional learning opportunities that are normally part of the early years in post?

In these respects, further discussion needs to take place as to what forms of longer term support are needed. This leads us to think that those who are planning similar initiatives should design longer term strategies than those that have been developed in this particular case. Furthermore, such strategies need to have a more detailed plan for the disengagement of the support that is to be provided by partners from other schools.

Final thoughts

The evidence from this study suggests that, under certain conditions, school to school cooperation offers a promising strategy for bringing about educational improvements in contexts where schools are facing difficulties. Indeed, it can be argued that it points towards a possible new direction for school improvement policy and practice more generally. It also shows that the practical involvement of experienced colleagues in the development of a newly appointed headteacher offers important strategies for growth to all parties. Not least interesting in our findings is the extent to which these experienced heads felt they, too, had grown through the experience.

MOVING LEADERSHIP PRACTICE IN SCHOOLS FORWARD

Samantha Fox and Mel Ainscow

How, then, can the idea of headteachers working together to foster improved leadership practice be taken forward? Based on collaborative research carried out by a 'think-tank' of experienced headteachers, this chapter explores the idea of action learning sets as a context for such developments. Members of the think-tank developed and analysed written accounts of interesting practice from the field, focusing particularly on urban schools that had addressed difficulties in behaviour among their student populations. Subsequently, a set of training materials was produced in order to guide groups of leaders in using the accounts of practice as part of leadership development programmes. While these approaches seem to be potentially powerful, their use on a wider basis presents a number of difficulties within a national policy context that demands rapid improvements.

Difficulties associated with student diversity are increasingly seen as a key challenge for educational leaders. This paper reports on the findings of a three-year project, carried out on behalf of the National College for School Leadership in England, that addresses this agenda. Conducted in partnership with practitioners, the study led to the development of an action learning strategy. The specific focus of the strategy is on the encouragement of forms of leadership that facilitate improvements in student behaviour – the issue that seems to be most challenging for many schools, particularly those serving economically poor urban districts.

In what follows, we provide an account of the project. In so doing, we draw out lessons about what actions might be useful in fostering forms of leadership that can help to create schools that are more effective in responding to student diversity. This leads us to discuss the difficulties of implementing such approaches within a policy context that is looking for solutions that can be implemented quickly across the education service.

Developing the strategy

Our study involved us in working in partnership with groups of school leaders. It focused specifically on the issue of how leadership might influence
student behaviour, a theme that had been determined as a priority among
practitioners by the National College for School Leadership. We started from
the assumption that the behaviour of students in schools should be understood in respect of their learning and the contexts in which learning is meant
to take place. This orientation is important in that it attempts to ensure that
the issue of behaviour is not perceived as being solely about the characteristics and circumstances of particular students. Rather, it opens up possibilities for analysing how school and community processes may be creating
barriers of various kinds that lead to negative responses among some learners.
Such an orientation locates the issue firmly within the agenda of school
improvement in a way that has direct implications for leadership.

The focus was, then, on the nature of leadership practice and how it
develops. Like Spillane and his colleagues (2001), the practitioners and
researchers involved in the study assumed that school leadership has to be
understood as a distributed practice, stretched over a school's social and
situational contexts. It was also assumed that the development of leadership
practice starts from personal experience and involves forms of social learning
as those within a given workplace explore ways of solving the practical problems they face as they carry out their duties (Copland 2003). Much of this
professional learning goes on at a largely intuitive level and the knowledge
that it creates is mainly unarticulated. In other words, those who develop
leadership skills find it difficult to describe the ways in which they do what
they do. It can be argued, therefore, that the most effective form of leadership
development is likely to be based within the workplace, using social learning
processes that influence thinking and action in a particular context.

In making sense of what this involves, we found it helpful to consider the
ideas of Etienne Wenger (1998), as discussed in Chapter 7, focusing specifically on the way he sees learning as 'a characteristic of practice'. He provides a
framework that can be used to analyse learning in social contexts. At the
centre of this framework is the concept of a 'community of practice', a social
group engaged in the sustained pursuit of a shared enterprise. Practices are, he
argues, ways of negotiating meaning through social action.

The study involved two phases as follows:

Phase 1: During the first two years of the study a think-tank of ten headteachers (five from primary schools and five from secondary), who were
interested in taking this agenda forward in their schools, met termly in order
to share ideas. Their discussions focused on the question: '*What forms of
leadership practice encourage behaviour that facilitates the learning of all students
within a school?*' During this period we acted as facilitators and critical friends
to the group, recording and interpreting the processes that took place. These
experiences showed how, under certain conditions, written 'accounts of
practice' can be used to stimulate a form of reflection that makes use of the
experience and knowledge that exists within a group of educational leaders.

They also showed how joint visits to schools in order to produce such accounts can have similar effects.

Phase 2: During the second phase of the study, four networks of schools (26 schools in total) used the materials and processes over a period of one year in order to review and develop their leadership practices. Heads and other senior staff from these schools formed local action learning groups, adopting a process similar to that used within the think-tank. Each group was facilitated and supported by a headteacher from the original think-tank. At the same time, the participants were encouraged to use the materials to facilitate a similar review and development process with leadership teams in their own schools.

Action learning

The approach used by the think-tank during the first phase of the study involved a participatory orientation along the lines of what has been defined as 'collaborative inquiry' (Reason and Rowan 1981; Reason 1988). More specifically, it took the form of 'action learning', a collaborative inquiry approach originally developed by Reg Revans, an English physicist (Bray et al. 2000). He recommended the creation of action learning 'sets', in other words, groups that work on solving real problems through repeated cycles of action and reflection. Such approaches emphasize the value of group processes and the use of varied methods of recording information. In this way, the action learning process experienced by the think-tank heads became the process by which their own leadership practices were challenged.

Over the two-year period, members of the think-tank developed and analysed written *accounts of practice* from the field, focusing particularly on schools (both primary and secondary) that had addressed difficulties in fostering more positive behaviour patterns among their student populations. These included a number of schools facing difficulties of one kind or another. The accounts were not seen as examples of 'good' practice, although each one included descriptions of practice that could be seen as being instructive.

Each account of practice was developed by at least two members of the think-tank. Together they visited a particular school where they carried out observations and interviews with students and staff. They also held meetings with senior staff in order to discuss their impressions. Initial drafts were then produced and these were amended in the light of comments from the schools.

One of the most significant features of the visits was the way in which colleagues from different schools supported one another in reviewing aspects of leadership practice. It was found that these linking activities had the potential to shed new light on familiar situations, both for the visitors and the visited. This adds support to other research suggesting that an engagement with evidence can, under certain conditions, help staff in schools to rethink their practices (Ainscow et al. in press). It involves the creation of 'interruptions' to the usual ways of thinking that exist within a school in order to create space and encouragement for reflection and mutual challenge. However, as we argued in Chapter 4, this is not in itself a straightforward mechanism for change. To have a chance to move practice forward, interruptions must be welcomed and they must follow an invitation to engage in dialogue.

With this in mind, links between schools were made on the basis that the visitors would be primarily going to assist the development of leadership practice in the host school by generating data and reflecting together on the possible implications. In this way, visitors went both as colleagues and as co-researchers, invited to find out more about the impact of existing practices.

Analysing leadership practice

The accounts of practice were used as a basis for discussion within the think-tank so as to draw together the experiences and knowledge of members of the group. Gradually, over a series of such discussions, eight interrelated themes emerged. The members of the think-tank concluded that these themes provided a useful framework for analysing leadership practice in relation to improvements in student behaviour. The themes are as follows:

1 *Understanding context*. Discussion of practice in a variety of settings drew attention to the importance of developing leadership practices that are sensitive to particular contexts. This underlines the importance of leaders collecting and engaging with forms of evidence that can deepen their understanding of the circumstances of a school, both internally and externally. While all schools are nowadays 'data rich', it is clear that some have better arrangements for using data for strategic purposes. In this respect, the use of various forms of qualitative data that enable school leaders to go behind the patterns provided by statistical evidence seems to be a particularly significant factor in contexts where improvements in behaviour occur. Such data enable groups of leaders to ask 'why' questions in order to determine new possibilities for moving policy and practice forward. Here the idea of listening to the voice of students seems to be a particularly powerful strategy. Indeed, there is considerable evidence that leaders who are sensitive to the views of students are in a stronger position for making effective strategic decisions about their schools. However, it also seems to be important that school leaders engage with sound evidence about external factors, such as community attitudes, that bear on the capacity of teachers to work successfully with students.
2 *The physical environment*. The analysis of accounts of schools within which there had been significant improvements in student behaviour drew attention to the importance of focusing on improvements in the physical environment within which teachers and students have to work. For example, heads who have been successful in 'turning round' schools in crisis often referred to immediate actions they had taken, such as painting corridors and reception areas, improving toilets, insisting on dress codes for students and staff and requiring students to bring necessary equipment.

Related to this is the apparent importance of creating a sense of identity within a school, through, for example, the use of a distinctive house-style for displays, notices and documentation. This seems to be associated with the creation of an image that encourages a feeling of being part of something particular that is instantly recognizable among students and staff, and, indeed, to those who visit the school. Such a strong sense of self-image is also seen as being important in relation to the 'selling' of the school to the wider community, a factor that is now regarded as being particularly critical within the context of the quasi-market that English schools are required to operate.

3 *Structures and systems.* Establishing procedures that create a sense of certainty seems to be an important factor, particularly in contexts where student behaviour has been significantly difficult. Thus, the introduction of clear policies in key areas, such as attendance, bullying or management responses to classroom incidents, seems to be associated with progress. However, having stated policies is only part of the answer. What matters most, it seems, is the extent to which such policies are turned into reality by consistent implementation over time. In one urban secondary school, for example, there is an established pattern that students are expected to sit where the teacher decides during lessons. These seating requirements are deliberately intended to encourage the integration of students across gender and ethnic divides. What is most striking is that the consistent implementation of this policy among all members of staff means that it is now taken for granted. Here, the importance of senior staff monitoring and insisting upon a high level of implementation seems to be a key factor.

4 *Leadership behaviour.* The issue of what leaders should spend their time doing is inevitably a key theme for consideration. Analysis of schools where there has been progress suggests that their actual presence around the school throughout the day is an important factor. In this way they are able to head off problems and support staff who may be experiencing difficulties, while at the same time modelling more positive ways of interacting with students. For example, the principal of one secondary school facing difficult circumstances described how she and members of her senior team visit every class a number of times each day. A primary school head explained that in many ways the morning assembly was a time for him to work with staff, since this provided opportunities to illustrate ways of engaging with children. Similarly, a secondary head explained how she stresses more or less the same points each morning in the staff briefing session. All of this contrasts with situations in which leaders become so involved in solving organizational and administrative problems that they find themselves unable to pay attention to such forms of 'management by walking about'. Some heads who appear to have had a positive influence on the learning climate in their schools express concern that their constant presence might lead to a sense of dependence among their colleagues. Others argue, however, that a period of relative dependence is necessary when confidence is low within a school. Only later, when certain patterns of behaviour are established, can staff be helped and encouraged to become more autonomous. Such discussions illustrate the

sense of dilemma faced by school leaders on a day to day basis, particularly those in difficult circumstances.

5 *Support.* The theme of providing support seemed to run through the discussions about how to improve behaviour within a school. It was also apparent in relation to different levels of organizational activity. It was noticeable, for example, that schools that improve behaviour seem to do so by strengthening the use of support for individual students. Here there are many possibilities, all of which seem to rest on the more effective use of human resources. It is important to note, of course, that what we mean by the 'staff of a school' now goes well beyond the team of teachers. Additional adults, such as teaching assistants and learning mentors, can all provide a means of giving greater support for individual learners in ways that can also make them feel more valued. Furthermore, such strategies strengthen a school's capacity to identify disputes and difficulties quickly in order that they do not grow into major incidents. For example, one secondary school has a team of supervisors, the members of which are available throughout the day in order to ensure a safe and supportive working atmosphere around the building. However, what seems clear is that presence of more adults is not in itself the answer. Rather, effective practice arises from forms of leadership that enable such additional human resources to work in a coordinated and appropriate way. In other words, those that are there to support also need support themselves.

6 *Cultural change.* As school heads discussed the issue of what forms of leadership practice is needed in order to foster more appropriate behaviour among students, there was frequent mention of the need to 'change the culture'. For example, those who had experienced success in this respect describe how they had transformed 'hearts and minds' among staff, students and families. In one primary school, that successfully integrates children whose disabilities mean that they can be highly disruptive, it is apparent that there is a collective will to share responsibility for finding ways of supporting the participation and learning of these students, such that both adults and children seem to step in instinctively to head off difficulties and prompt more appropriate behaviours. In this particular school there is evidence of a powerful form of social learning that has an influence on the attitudes and conduct of everybody involved. This can be contrasted with schools in which members of staff describe how some of their colleagues walk along the corridor looking away when there is a disruptive incident. Once such attitudes become common within a school they too create a process of social learning such that everybody becomes largely preoccupied with looking after themselves. The million-dollar question, of course, is, how *can* leaders change school culture? A number of heads stressed the importance of working directly with the students themselves, convincing them that the school is improving and that this is to their advantage. In this way, it is argued, changes in student attitude and behaviour can be used as a lever to bring about changes in staff attitudes and behaviour.

7 *Sustainability.* The idea of cultural change draws attention to the issue of sustainability. This seems to be a particular problem in the current English

educational environment, where national reform policies tend to emphasize 'quick fix' solutions, with short-term improvement targets and planning cycles. A theme that is stressed by heads is the need for persistence. In other words, certain ideas have to be stressed as being fundamental to the school's longer term improvement strategy and that whatever happens these will not go away. Such ideas have to go beyond simple rhetoric into ways that will influence behaviour of adults and children on a day to day manner. So, for example, the head of an urban secondary school with a strong commitment to notions of inclusion tells her staff almost every day, 'smile and let-on to people that you pass in the corridor'. Of course, she herself endorses this policy by her own behaviour around the school. Again there is a sharp contrast here with those schools in which the visitor is greeted by the sound of a member of staff yelling at students who are wearing their shirts outside their trousers.

8 *Imperatives.* Clearly as school leaders concentrate their efforts on improvements in behaviour and learning within their organizations they cannot afford to lose track of external factors that bear on their work. In this sense so much of what is going on has the potential to provide perverse incentives that can discourage the developments of those practices that could improve working relationships among staff and students. We have already noted the impact of short-term planning and performance targets. Other potentially negative factors, within the English policy context, include: the aggregating of performance data that may encourage some staff to sacrifice certain groups of students in order to improve overall test or examination scores in their department; open enrolment, such that heads feel the need to act in ways that will attract students from certain types of home background; and the fragmenting of different national policies, such that resources are wasted and opportunities for significant improvement are missed. Having said that, it is also the case that some schools do seem to develop ways of working that seem to minimize these potential dangers and, in so doing, are able to turn what appear as external threats into opportunities for moving policies and practices forward. Much of this seems to be associated with strategic analysis in order to develop an improvement plan that joins together different agendas and resources; and co-operative problem-solving within which different members of a school community, including relevant outsiders, use their different experiences and perspectives in order define the best way forward.

These eight themes are, then, a summary of the collective conclusions of the headteachers that were involved in the first phase of the project. There was also strong evidence that the strategy that had evolved had had a powerful influence on their thinking and practice. They talked with enthusiasm about a professional development process that they saw as being tailored to their interests. In most cases they also talked about specific ways in which they and their senior management teams had changed their practices as a direct result of their involvement in the project. Many of them felt confident that these changes had led to improvements in relationships and behaviour within their school communities. This led us to feel optimistic that our strategy could be of benefit to other schools and other groups of school leaders.

Widening involvement

As a result of the findings of the collaborative research carried out by the think-tank, a set of materials was produced in order to guide other groups of leaders who wished to use the accounts as the basis for leadership development. These materials focus on ten accounts of practice. They also provide an overall review framework for thinking about leadership within a school based on the eight themes described above. In addition, the materials include literature extracts that are intended to be used to:

- *further stimulate reflection* by enabling the reader to compare what they do with accounts of leadership practice elsewhere;
- *challenge and reframe existing thinking* by reading evidence about leadership practices that have proved to be successful in other contexts; and
- *conceptualize learning* through engagement with texts that provide deeper theoretical explanations of what is involved in leadership practice.

The development materials are intended to be used by groups of leaders within schools, or from a group of schools, in order to foster yet further action learning activities of the sort that took place within the think-tank. The central aim is to encourage groups of colleagues to work together in order to move thinking and practice forward within their organizations.

The starting point for the work of such an action learning group is the existing experience and knowledge of its members. Those taking part must, therefore, be helped to take responsibility for their own learning. Colleagues in the group are seen as sources of challenge and support, bringing their experiences and perspectives to the discussions that take place. Within such contexts written accounts of practice, plus the additional readings, are used to stimulate reflection and creativity. Emphasis is placed on social learning processes, using different perspectives as a stimulus and a resource (the interrelated nature of these processes is illustrated in Figure 9.1).

Using the development materials, the second phase of the study provided an opportunity to test out the transferability of the strategy, focusing on issues such as: can the processes and materials be transferred to other leadership groups? Does their use within such a group effect change? Are there other contextual factors in relation to the particular groups that have an effect on the success of the process?

The four networks of schools involved at that stage monitored their work in relation to a common evaluation framework, focusing on: *process* (for example, what have we learnt about using the materials effectively?) and *outcomes* (for example, to what extent have these processes led to changes in behaviour among adults and students?) Again, external support was provided in order to ensure that this evaluation was carried out with suitable rigour.

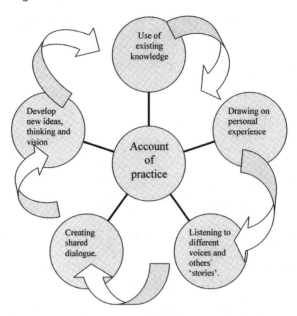

Figure 9.1 The elements of the leadership development strategy

Applying the strategy

The four networks were selected by their willingness to give time to the project. Two of the groups consisted of leaders from primary schools and two involved secondary schools. Chosen from different geographical areas across the UK, the schools all served urban communities characterized by factors typically associated with high socioeconomic deprivation. Several of the schools were either in, or had recently been in special measures, a formal category used to designate schools that are seen to be failing as a result of inspection. All four groups were looking for ways to promote mutual support between schools in response to what they saw as a lack of collaboration within their local education authorities.

While the materials were intended to be used flexibly to suit different circumstances, the experience of the think-tank had pointed to certain steps that were seen to be helpful. These were as follows:

1 The group of leaders discuss the themes and questions in the review framework in relation to the overall question: 'What forms of leadership practice encourage behaviour that facilitates the learning of all students within a school?' The group then choose an 'account of practice' that seems to be relevant to their interests.
2 Individual members of the group read the selected account, making notes of issues and ideas that it brings to mind about their own workplace and practices.
3 At a meeting of the group, the account is analysed using the experiences of

individuals in their schools to inform the discussion. An external facil-
itator acts as chair, and care is taken to ensure that all individuals contribute. In the case of a larger group (i.e., more than eight members) small
group discussion can be used prior to whole group debate.

4 After a period of discussion, members of the group are invited to read the
'focused texts'. These are carefully chosen extracts from relevant articles or
books. The intention is that these texts will help the group to reconsider
the account in ways that may draw attention to overlooked possibilities for
moving thinking and practice forward.

5 The group reviews the discussion, focusing specifically on practices within
their schools that need to be addressed. Where possible, action learning
partnerships are created to support development activities.

Further cycles of action learning are then planned, using other accounts to
stimulate discussions. In due course, members of the group visit one another's
schools in order to generate their own accounts of practice. Such visits are
intended to 'make the familiar unfamiliar' in ways that stimulate self-questioning, creativity and action.

Each of the four networks was encouraged to follow this sequence of steps
over a period of almost a year. Their discussions were facilitated by a member
of the original think-tank, who also supported group members in thinking
about how they might lead similar activities with colleagues in their own
schools.

In the event, the nature of what occurred in each of the networks varied
considerably, reflecting local history and circumstances, the biographies of
the people involved, social relationships within the groups and, of course, the
personal style of each of the external facilitators. In some instances the levels
of collaboration between group members, while being cordial, remained at a
relatively superficial level. As a result, more challenging agendas remained
largely untouched. On the other hand, elsewhere we saw examples of how
groups gradually developed a willingness to surface their worries and think
aloud with colleagues they appeared to trust about how these issues might be
addressed. Mutual school visits were found to be particularly helpful in fostering such engagement, thus reinforcing the positive experiences of the visits
carried out during phase one.

Engaging with this social complexity is helpful in drawing out the lessons
of the experiences. Here the concept of communities of practice, referred to
earlier, is a helpful starting point. This is a notion which sees practice as the
product of a particular group of people who continuously negotiate and
renegotiate practice on the basis of meanings, beliefs and values that are
broadly shared but within which conflicts and disagreements can arise.
Externally designed strategies, such as the one we have outlined in this
chapter, are implemented through such communities. However, in their
implementation they are imbued with the particular meanings given to them
by each community and may, on some occasions, be changed beyond
recognition.

The notion of communities of practice is one of a family of approaches to
understanding organized human endeavour that have arisen in reaction to

functionalist views of organizations (Burrell and Morgan 1979). Such approaches distrust the idea that organizations emerge as rationally designed responses to self-evident problems and tasks. Instead, they stress the ways in which organizations emerge within particular sets of social conditions and reflect the assumptions, values and power relations which characterize those conditions. The tasks social groups set themselves, the problems they identify, the tools they devise to carry our their work, the forms and structures within which they organize themselves, are all shaped by the social conditions within which they live – the implication being that social groups living under different conditions will see their worlds differently and will set themselves different tasks to be tackled in different ways and within different forms of organization.

These postfunctionalist perspectives play a powerful role since they help us to call into question the inevitability and rationality of traditional forms of schooling which result in practices that make some students feel marginalized. What these perspectives add is an analysis not only of the way in which purposeful activity is shaped by the cultural resources (understandings, values, tools and so on) which particular social groups can bring to bear on their tasks, but also of the social processes through which such resources are developed and deployed.

The implication is that if we are to understand how our four groups of school leaders responded to the invitation to reflect upon and develop their practices, we would need to understand more about both the cultural resources which were available in their working contexts, the social relations between members of the school communities and, indeed, the wider relations and structures of society as a whole.

Such a detailed, close-up investigation of context was, unfortunately, far beyond the scope of this investigation and this represents a severe limitation in what we are able to report. Nevertheless, the evidence we have confirms the view that the processes that occurred in the four groups were strongly influenced by factors at the local level. This means, of course, that the sustainability of the strategy we were developing was under question due to the particular facilitation skills required to orchestrate the social learning processes involved. In particular, it required external consultants who, with very little time available, had to somehow make sense of, and take account of, a range of interconnected local factors that had a bearing on what they were trying to achieve.

Conclusion

Our research leaves us feeling cautiously optimistic. It suggests that when groups of school leaders develop more collaborative ways of working of the sort we have described, this can have an impact on how they perceive themselves and their work. Specifically, comparisons of practice within and between schools can lead them to rethink their aspirations, not least in relation to the way they view students whose behaviour seems to challenge the status quo. Rather than simply presenting problems that are assumed to be insurmountable, such students may come to be perceived as providing feedback on existing arrangements. In this way they may be seen as sources of understanding as to how these arrangements might be developed in ways that could be of benefit to the whole school community.

However, by their nature such approaches are difficult to introduce and sustain, not least because they tend to disrupt existing assumptions and well-established ways of working. This being the case, there is a need to foster both support and challenge within such action learning groups. Our research points to the following factors that seem to be important in this respect:

- *Commitment*: Progress requires a commitment from group members to the group as well as to the process. There is also a need to recognize that the processes involved require a commitment over time in order that they can be effective. In other words, it has to be understood that this is not a 'quick fix'.
- *Willingness*: Alongside this sense of commitment there is a need for those involved to be prepared to have at least an open mind about the materials and to be prepared to follow the model of adult learning involved.
- *Relationships*: It follows that much of this is about relationships. In particular, the forms of self-questioning that are involved require a degree of openness and trust among group members.
- *Agreed purposes*: Motivation seems to arise from a sense that the processes involved will have a pay off for individuals. This is why it is essential that areas of focus are negotiated and agreed within the group.
- *Power*: Such negotiations will sometimes lead to tensions, as different group members argue their corners with respect to their own priorities and interests. This is why, in our experience, it is better to have groups within which there are members who have a similar status.

Together these five factors underline the challenge facing those who take on the task of facilitating action learning groups. Our research suggests that it is helpful if such facilitators are experienced educational leaders themselves, that they are from outside the particular working contexts, and that they have themselves experienced the processes involved as participants in similar development activities.

Bearing this advice in mind, we believe that the findings outlined in this chapter provide the basis of an approach to leadership development that can make a significant difference in the field. This suggests that the way forward is to develop 'communities of practice' that can stimulate reflection and mutual learning among groups of school leaders. This implies the negotiation of new relationships that will encourage interdependent learning among groups of educational leaders within a local context. The problem is that such approaches do not lend themselves to the idea of 'scaling up', as it is generally defined (Tobin 2005). Consequently, they do not fit easily into a national strategy that demands system-wide measures that can be 'delivered' by intermediaries. Our contention is that such requirements act as a barrier to the development of more powerful strategies of the sort we have outlined.

COLLABORATION WITH A CITY-WIDE PURPOSE: MAKING PATHS FOR SUSTAINABLE EDUCATIONAL IMPROVEMENT

Andy Howes and Mel Ainscow

Staying with the theme of interdependence, this chapter reports on a study of a city LEA in which efforts have been made to encourage all of its secondary schools to work collaboratively. This leads its authors to conclude that there is a potentially powerful role for cluster arrangements, which in some cases influenced core processes within individual schools. In addition, the chapter examines the impact of the involvement of a private partner in the early stages of the initiative. It involved brokering, providing space and capacity building in the LEA. This changed a long-term dynamic in the LEA, while also creating hostility among headteachers and teachers, some of whom argue that the same improvements could have been achieved more effectively and ethically by giving the funding direct to schools. The chapter concludes with a review of opportunities and barriers that exist when attempting to use collaboration to bring about system-wide reform.

For many policymakers, it is an unwelcome yet unavoidable truth that school autonomy within an environment of competition and choice has not brought about significant improvements for all learners in economically poorer urban contexts. In accepting this fact, some government and other policymakers have been looking to collaboration within networks of schools as a way of embedding school improvement more deeply.

Over recent years, people working in quite different contexts have recognized the advantages of formalized networks. For example, Wohlstetter et al. (2003) studied school networks in Los Angeles and found that the systematic decentralization of resources and power enhanced the capacity of individual schools to reform. In the UK context, interschool networking has been encouraged by the National College for School Leadership, and some clear benefits have been seen, but the influence of the dominant competition agenda has meant that not all of this networking is collaborative (Busher and

Hodgkinson 1996), and it has not often been demonstrably effective in raising pupil attainment across schools.

Where collaboration between schools becomes meaningful, it involves opportunities such as the sharing of problem solving and development associated with particularly talented teachers and leaders (Hargreaves 2003), and for a spreading of the distinctive areas of strength that schools build up because of the particularities of their student intake and links with other agencies (Ainscow et al. in press). The value of collaboration partly depends on whether or not resources which are found to facilitate educational improvement in one school are available and useful to others. Proponents of collaboration suggest that there are very few schools with nothing to learn from others, and with nothing to offer to them.

Collaboration in a diverse urban context must, it seems, be about improving the challenging conditions in which many headteachers must create change – not with the unrealistic expectation of a level educational playing field, but in finding ways to add to the sources of support and challenge that headteachers and middle leaders can rely on. Setting up such collaboration demands a level-headed appreciation of some key conditions, such as allowing sufficient time for the relatively slow process of building mutual trust through appropriate shared risks and responsibilities. The reality and implications of this are illuminated in the case study at the heart of this chapter.

The context

Much of the literature on collaboration underplays the significance of local context, although there is some research to suggest that what goes on at the district level has a significant role to play in respect of processes of school improvement (e.g. Elmore 2004). This chapter is a result of a two-year study of a city-wide improvement process which made collaboration, within four networks of secondary schools, the main route to sustainable higher achievement. The study was carried out on behalf of the DfES.

Since collaboration is essentially a social process, we felt that it was important to pay attention to the various perspectives of those involved, including teachers and other members of staff, school leaders, local authority officers and the private company working with them – and to observe and reflect on how they worked together in pursuit of the objectives. Our conclusions are drawn from variations in responses to this process in the various collaborative groupings. These variations suggest that the necessary negotiation of interdependent relationships between schools, local authorities and their wider communities requires increasingly skilful and considered approaches from leaders at all levels in the system. The evidence of this study supports the idea that this is particularly true in the general context of competing educational agendas and uncertainty about forms of governance.

Certainly, some features of the local educational context at the beginning of this process were relatively unconducive to the establishment of systematic and sustainable collaborative working. City schools had long competed for pupils on the basis of reputations and particularly pupil attainment outcomes. Relatively low expectations of students were widespread. At transition to secondary school, student migration was widespread as more engaged parents sought out places in relatively high attaining schools. Falling rolls required the closure of two secondary schools in the first two years of the project. More positively however, a strong existing partnership set up as a result of the national Excellence in Cities (EiC) initiative was well-integrated into the leadership structures of schools and local authority, with over 50 learning mentors in place in schools and many 'gifted and talented' students taking advantage of additional educational opportunities. In addition, major staff changes in the local authority's secondary school improvement team had resulted in a new and more focused approach to challenging schools. The first newsletter to schools about the project described in this chapter spoke of building on

> the real successes of schools and LEA over the past four years. The partnership brings additional support and, we hope, some innovative strategies for improvement. But at the same time we want to build on the successful relations built between schools and the LEA, real improvements in literacy and numeracy across the city, the benefits of programmes developed within EiC, the emerging Behaviour Support plan and many other strong features already in place across the City.
>
> (May 2002)

From the perspective of one senior LEA officer, EiC was a necessary but not sufficient element in bringing about change in ownership of the improvement agenda:

> We couldn't have got where we are without EiC, but EiC alone couldn't have done it.

In making sense of collaboration we found it helpful to use the metaphor of *creating new paths for improvement* – with headteachers and others constructing these paths as they travelled together. Once made, these paths make further improvement easier, since they facilitate the continued purposeful working together of school leaders, local authority representatives and external agencies. This was a development which effectively harnessed new energy from the school system, creating new forms of governance and accountability based on the development and consolidation of school to school partnerships of various forms. Changes in ethos depended on a release of goodwill and an extension of trust which was hard to anticipate at the start.

We come to a generally positive conclusion about the role that collaboration played in creating paths for improvement in this case. Over a relatively short period, secondary schools in the city demonstrated how collaborative arrangements can provide an effective means of solving immediate problems, such as staff shortages; how they can have a positive impact during periods of crisis, such as during the closure of a school; and how, in the longer run, schools working together can contribute to the raising of aspirations and attainment in schools that have had a record of low achievement. The data show that attainment levels increased between 2002 and 2004 in all four school groupings, and the trends indicated by KS3 results suggest that they will continue to do so over the next few years. There was also strong evidence that collaboration helped reduce the polarization of the education system to the particular benefit of those pupils who are on the edges of the system and performing relatively poorly, although impact was uneven.

Of course, none of what we say applies across the board – each of the 18 secondary schools and the people maintaining and developing them had their own orientations, ethos and context, and it would be arrogant to assume that their intentions, capabilities and achievements can be summed up in a few pages. Nevertheless, we will attempt to draw out some lessons to be learnt from this example that are of value to others labouring towards similar goals.

The project

Briefly, the project described here involved the construction of four groups of secondary schools within an English city education authority. Additional DfES funding (in excess of £1 million) was provided to support the process and a private company was hired to work alongside the local authority in setting up the project. Whole-hearted participation in the project could not be mandated; however, the assumption was that all city secondary schools would participate. In practice, most schools were enthused by the prospect of collaborating in small groups, but a minority of schools were less willing.

A steering group was set up to manage the project. This included the director of education and key officers, representative headteachers, experienced staff from another local authority, senior DfES advisers and staff from the private company. On a day to day basis, the core project team consisted of just two people: a member of the private company (himself a highly regarded local ex-headteacher) and a local authority officer working full-time on the initiative. Early on, the private company played an essential role in creating additional capacity for brokering between schools.

Headteachers were consulted extensively over the school groupings, which were organized not on geographical proximity but in order to bring together schools at different stages of development and with varied levels of examination success. Representatives from schools in another local authority with a history of collaborative working were attached to each grouping.

The basic project design featured a 'twin-track' approach. The first track involved short-term initiatives aiming to assist schools in raising standards for all students; particularly to meet the government's 'floor target' requirements within two years, according to which all schools were to have at least 25 percent of their Year 11 pupils attaining five or more A* to C GCSE grades. These initiatives included the production of revision guides in some subjects, booster classes for students just under the attainment targets and rapid introduction of alternative courses taught with additional staffing in key areas. Some of these initiatives were put in place through coordination between schools at subject level. Unusually, staff were paid additional money for attending project meetings out of school. These activities were promoted through collaborative structures and encouraged some sharing of ideas and experiences. However, they entailed very little collaboration between staff in schools.

The second track was a longer term strategy based on strengthening collaboration among the city's schools. As a relatively small local authority, the city's education department was seen to have insufficient resources to meet all the development needs of schools without input from expertise already located in the schools. Collaboration was intended to facilitate more sharing of resources than had proved possible under earlier schemes, such as the Beacon schools initiative. The implication too was that changing relationships between schools would gradually be mirrored by changing relationships with officers of the education department. With this in mind, a school improvement adviser was allocated to work with each school grouping.

How collaboration developed

Significantly, the four school groupings developed in quite different ways, reflecting differences in context and history. It is helpful to briefly describe these differences here, highlighting one or two significant developments in each case.

Group A

Group A consisted of only four schools: a strong traditional foundation school, a school that had reopened after failing to improve following inspection, one newly opened school and one marked for closure. They were geographically closer than those in the other school groupings and a particularly close collaboration developed through the sharing of resources. Headteachers decided to manage the group directly to ensure that activities fitted in with existing school development priorities. They quickly learned that they could rely on each other for support and challenge:

> The project takes pressure off people ... Knowing that you can ring someone ... galvanizes you to do things sometimes'
>
> (Headteacher)

At this stage, while encouraging collaboration as a general principle, the group only involved teachers where it fulfilled a strategic need that they had identified.

A critical stage for this group concerned the closure of one of the four schools in July 2004 and the takeover of the buildings by the strong school – which could have caused great conflict. In practice, the help given by the group resulted in the school's final cohort attaining more highly than their predecessors in previous years. This is significant in that often school closures lead key staff to move on, leaving the feeling of a sinking ship. The school grouping helped to avoid this by creating a sense of continuity, working together on joint projects, sharing resources and requiring staff newly appointed to the group to work in the school for the first year of their contract. The head of the school noted that 'we were able to get at a field of staff which we couldn't get at before'. Significantly too, the closing school continued to offer some resources in return. The other headteachers were a ready source of support and advice for him ('I'll go to them much quicker than to the LEA if I have an issue') and he was able to offer strong teachers in subjects such as art to work part-time in the other schools, to everyone's benefit.

A lot was learnt from this process. The headteacher of the traditional school now talks of 'bussing by consent', describing the possibilities for creating a good social mix in all the schools in the group. There is an important ethnic dimension to this, which suggests that increased collaboration among schools may be an important way of tackling the ethnic divide built up between schools in the city.

Group B

Group B successfully developed a sustainable working pattern as a result of a struggle to be more strategic about collaboration for improvement. The five secondary schools, together with another partner from the linked LEA, all worked in different contexts and with varied average levels of attainment. The headteachers decided quickly that they were committed to the project and to each other, prioritizing their meetings, speaking openly about difficulties, focusing increasingly on teaching and learning, and contributing substantial funds to a communal pot. The decision to appoint and pay for a coordinator at the level of deputy headteacher was critical in creating greater capacity for sustained collaboration after the end of the funded project.

One school was in the special measures category, and they benefited from this pot: as the headteacher remarked, 'our thanks to the other schools for the financial support for continuing collaboration – it is extraordinary'. Interestingly again, the school in trouble contributed significantly to the group. In this case, their inspection-driven focus on teaching and learning influenced the other schools to pay more direct attention to classroom processes. All schools had skilful teachers who actively assisted counterpart departments in other schools in the group. This process began through an orchestrated training day and continued through individual contact, encouraged by school leaders.

The group coordinator was involved in making connections, such as facilitating support for particular teachers at the struggling school and linking up with initiatives that were otherwise seen as 'innovation overload'. However, her role was full of uncertainty, going beyond institutional structures and resulting in periodic dilemmas as to where she should place her effort. She, more than anyone, grappled with the question, 'How do we set something up which is sustainable?' It was this struggle which led to a group application for a different government initiative (i.e. Leading Edge) and a consequent reshaping of stated priorities, while maintaining the significant relationships that the group had built.

Group C

Group C comprised five schools, one of which was a new style 'city academy', another that had already become successful in improving achievement among learners from disadvantaged backgrounds and three that were in challenging circumstances. Collaboration in this group was first and foremost a mechanism for brokering effectively with externally available resources. A particular focus was the 14 to 19 curriculum, and the production of joint resources for revision and supported self-study. Progress was impeded, however, by the (frustrated) expectation that all schools would participate. One headteacher in particular chose not to engage with the project, saying that it did not address real problems and that leaders of schools in challenging circumstances did not have time for planning meetings.

Only once the group agreed to appoint a coordinator was there a significant push forward with activities. As the coordinator said:

> I'm making myself the focus for their loyalty. I'm the person who will be banging on the door complaining if they don't do what they said they would. I'm encouraging them to take part.

The experience of this group supported the argument that collaboration requires the commitment of key stakeholders, and that self-interest is, in practice, a predictable and important component of interdependency. This suggests that a necessary (but not sufficient) condition for a successful large-scale intervention based on collaboration is an appeal to self-interest and not simply to altruism.

Group D

Group D included five secondary schools, four of which were 'facing challenging circumstances' and one of which, at the outset of the project, had been placed in 'special measures' by the government school inspection service, Ofsted. The fifth school was a large, highly successful voluntary aided school affiliated to a large church. There was also a special school linked to the group. Collaborative activities were slow to materialize within the grouping, but the sense of imposition was a mainly positive factor:

> It was imposed on us, otherwise we certainly would not have seen it as a priority. But you can't make the gelling happen.

New headteachers were appointed to three of the five schools over the period of the project and this slowed down collaboration but did not prevent it. Initial activities were well-received but unfocused. Gradually, however, initiatives involving the sharing of resources between schools took shape. One example concerns English teaching, where the headteachers together paid for and managed a shared member of staff:

> We realized in a group meeting that we were all in dire straits in English. Only one school had a head of English. The headteacher there said 'I've got an excellent teacher who is looking to move'. Our LEA adviser knew the teacher, and she managed and facilitated the appointment. It is a

middle leader post, and we four schools interested share a quarter of the cost

(Headteacher)

This was a strategic development for schools whose relatively patchy reputation was making it impossible for them to appoint suitably qualified teachers. It was repeated in other subjects, such as music where three schools were *unable* to offer music because of a lack of qualified staff, while another school in the group had more than ten music teachers. The group tackled the problem through another initiative to share resources, and coordinated a joint link with influential institutions beyond school in a way that individual schools would find impossible.

Drawing the lessons

A comparison of changing results at GCSE, together with an understanding of what processes were taking place in schools through the project, suggest strongly that there was a positive impact on pupil attainment. It is impossible to be sure that this would not have occurred without collaboration, but previous years' results suggest that this is unlikely.

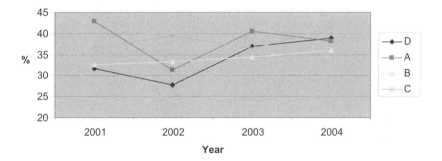

Figure 10.1 % 5A–C at GCSE by school group

The striking observation from these four brief accounts is how the school groupings that developed from this city-wide project quickly became quite distinctive. In what follows, key aspects of these processes are compared and contrasted in order to deepen understanding of the nature and impact of collaboration. This analysis is structured in relation to five propositions that emerge from the comparison of the four cases:

1 *Collaboration has promoted wider ownership of the improvement agenda.* This has been part of a process whereby more individual schools and more groups of schools have felt a stake in the process of school improvement. As a result, they have found themselves able to act together in various combinations to tackle complex and deep-rooted problems in schools.

2 *Collaboration has contributed to changes in practice.* The accounts reveal how collaborating schools have contributed to a wide range of improvements, whether in terms of resources for teaching and learning; the provision and preparation of teachers and other staff; the development of alternative curricula and activities; or the measures used to determine successful teaching.

3 *However, collaboration does not in itself generate a clear picture of good practice that teachers can work with.* Our evidence indicates that collaboration alone own does not provide the models for development, and the accounts show that when groups of schools are planning new developments, the stimulus of materials and ideas from other sources (such as the national KS3 strategy and others) was extremely important.

4 *Collaboration does not in itself create sufficient challenge for improvement.* There was an ongoing issue in relation to sources of challenge. It proved difficult for collaborating headteachers, working hard to share resources and build relationships, to address the pressing needs, either of individual schools or within the system, without the assistance of outsiders to the group. The four cases demonstrate how important the role of local authority staff can be in this regard.

5 *But collaboration helps to ensure that tensions created by improvement initiatives are held in balance.* What collaboration did do was to help reduce the polarization of the education system, to the particular benefit of those pupils on the edges of the system and performing relatively poorly. Since collaboration was about active involvement of staff from different schools, there was a constant interaction at a level which was close to practice and to the context that schools are working in every day. Consequently, staff see and understand each others' issues much more clearly, and are able to contribute to resolving the tensions that necessarily arise with the implementation of improvement plans.

These propositions are supported by evidence from interviews and observations, some of which is detailed below.

Wider ownership of the improvement agenda

During the early phase of the project, the private partner played an important role in the dynamics of these changes. We saw how the project team gained a high profile in the authority, earning the respect of senior local authority staff on the one hand, and most of the headteachers on the other. A few headteachers argued that they could have developed the strategy, without outside involvement, if the available finance had been made available to them. Our own view was that the recent history of the local authority provided little support for such an assertion. Indeed, the evidence was that the strong schools were getting stronger, while the lower performing schools were falling behind at an alarming rate, and that a culture of blame had developed between schools and local authority staff as to where the problems lay.

Given this context, the development of school groups represented a movement away from a relatively stuck culture towards a growing recognition that many problems are not entirely beyond the influence of schools and groups of schools working together. This shift was associated with a much-improved relationship between the LEA and schools. Reflecting on the impact of the project, the LEA director emphasized the importance of developing ownership of the challenge to improve:

> Because the project has primarily been about raising standards above floor targets, it has helped develop the sense that we're all in the job together and co-own the school improvement agenda. We're conscious that grouping schools together in the school groupings has given schools the confidence and the forum to speak together about issues that are causing them concern – an example would be admissions arrangements. The school grouping structure and the 'peer' support that it has nurtured has enabled us to say to weaker schools that they should be seeking solutions to problems within their own capacity/school grouping, rather than always relying on the LEA
>
> (Director of education)

By emphasizing ownership by different stakeholders, the director was drawing attention to the new possibilities that exist in a local authority when there are strong partnerships between schools. New forms of support are created, and new conversations become possible about responsibility for improvement. Again here, the metaphor of making paths for improvement seems useful and powerful.

Significantly, the local authority itself changed in response to the collaborative structures. Many senior staff in schools reported that dialogue and joint problem solving had become strong features of the relationship between officers and schools – and this was largely the outcome of working through disagreements. For example, in March 2004, local authority staff made moves to try to change the school groupings to become more geographical. The headteachers in one of the school groupings were in favour of such a move, seeing it as being in their interests. However, another group of headteachers went 'en masse' to an LEA strategy meeting and made it very clear that they would reject any such proposal. In so doing, they further reinforced their identity as a group of schools and as a power to be reckoned with. The LEA accepted their position and, in so doing, found that this in itself opened up new possibilities. One local authority officer expressed satisfaction with

> strong school groupings, if there really is co-ownership of the school improvement agenda ... All it does is to mean you need better arguments for what you want to do. And you get the energy of these headteachers, focused on school improvement. That's wonderful.

He illustrated this with a concrete example:

> What I have done, on the back of this discussion, is to go back to the group and say, 'OK, if you're that strong, can you work together to sort out the issue of inclusion?' They all said yes, in principle, they would accept over the admissions limit.

All of this echoes the evidence of other school improvement research that has drawn attention to the way periods of 'turbulence' arise as attempts are made to change the status quo (Hopkins et al. 1994). Turbulence may take a number of different forms, involving organizational, psychological, technical or micropolitical dimensions. At its heart, however, it is about the dissonance that occurs as experienced practitioners struggle to make sense of new ideas and new ways of working. It is interesting to note, too, that there is evidence to suggest that without a period of turbulence, successful, long-lasting change is unlikely to occur. In this sense, turbulence can be seen as a useful indication that schools are, indeed, on the move. The question is, of course, whether those involved in such processes are skilful and experienced enough to cope with such periods of difficulty.

Changes in practice

Mapping the key processes identified through the accounts in this way, suggests a useful shorthand for understanding the nature of the different changes that took place and the timescale for their impact (see Figure 10.2).

DIRECT IMPACT◄────────────────────────────►LONGER TERM IMPACT

Movement of human resources

    Joint advertisements/appointments

        Staff development activities

            Widening opportunities for pupils

                Drawing new resources

                    Mutual challenge

                        Re-defining quality

                            Shared responsibility

Figure 10.2 Changes in practice: mapping key processes

Those activities with a more direct and immediate impact on achievement tended to be *relatively* easy to implement. However, the accounts also demonstrate how, in the longer run, collaboration can help to foster more complex initiatives that may well contribute to sustainable improvements. Ideally this would lead to a commitment to particular values and, eventually, a sense of shared responsibility for the progress of all the students within a network.

In Group A, there was evidence that working practices started to reshape parental choices around the schools involved; and in Group B, the issue of priorities for development were comprehensively addressed through fine targeting in the strategic plan. Schools in Group C looked to other collaborative groups for longer term effects. In Group D, debates among headteachers moved on to focus on the question, 'What are our values?'

The records of meetings and discussions in the school groupings show that the direction of changes in the practice of teaching and learning came not just from the group, but from initiatives and other resources that the group were able to access. Examples from all four school grouping accounts bear this out.

The local officer in charge of the lower secondary improvement programme (KS3 strategy) encouraged the school groupings to use the strategy as a tool, inviting them to take advantage of the subject leader training and middle management programmes. Interestingly, the 2004 test results make the city the most improved LEA in the country at KS3. A range of other initiatives in subjects such as enterprise education, music and creative arts were all used by school groupings to give direction and coherence to collaborative developments in practice.

From an early stage there was evidence in some of the school groupings of a critical edge to discussions about priorities and what they really needed to address. However, as one local officer explained, sometimes 'within school groupings, the primary thing is to preserve the harmony of the group'. In some cases explicit challenges were apparent, but this has not been easy to achieve. So, for example, peer review among groups of heads proved difficult to engage in initially. However, peer review *supported by local authority officers* was eventually carried out in all groups, and widely seen as a useful and productive process.

Collaboration involves working not with an abstract or distant model of 'good practice', but rather learning directly from neighbouring schools what is possible in the context of the inevitable tensions and compromises with which school leaders and teachers have to deal. The stories of the four groups show how headteachers with different priorities tended to emphasize different resolutions of these tensions, and how these differences can be very productive. The different levels of provision for lower and higher attaining pupils in schools in Group A, for example, led to productive exchange of resources and mutual learning, and eventually to a systematic widening of the curriculum on offer through course places for pupils from the other schools. In Group B, the direct link with the special school led to developmental work on areas that might otherwise have received little attention in the push for targets.

As we saw, in two of the school groupings coordinators played an important role in sustaining improvement efforts in the context of competing pressures. It was noticeable, for example, how they were able to create momentum through particular projects, seeking out opportunities and building allegiances. On some occasions, they were seen to hold back where they judged attempts to engage in collaborative effort to be counterproductive. This leads us to argue that collaboration for school improvement requires someone who can take challenges to a headteacher, or group of headteachers, and, at the same time, maintain a forward-looking dialogue that helps to expand horizons beyond the individual school.

Conclusion

The evidence of this study points to certain conditions that are necessary in order to make school to school collaboration effective. These are as follows:

- The presence of incentives that encourage key stakeholders to explore the possibility that collaboration will be in their own interests;
- Headteachers and other senior staff in schools who are willing and skilful enough to drive collaboration forward towards collective responsibility, coping with the inevitable uncertainties and turbulence;
- The creation of common improvement agendas that are seen to be relevant to a wide range of stakeholders;
- Coherent external support from credible consultants/advisers (from the local authority or elsewhere) who have the confidence to learn alongside their school-based partners, exploring and developing new roles and relationships where necessary.

Collaboration of the type described in this chapter suggests that there is a potentially powerful role for cluster arrangements which in some cases exert a positive influence on core processes within individual schools. There is also evidence that the commitment of headteachers to collaboration can draw in other staff, provided that there are appropriate structures and processes in place. However, the evidence also shows that the successful use of school to school collaboration is far from straightforward, particularly within the English context, where competition and choice continue to be the driving forces of national education policy.

All of this leads us to conclude that national policymakers would be naive to overlook the influence of what happens at the local authority level. This is particularly so in urban contexts, where local history, interconnections between schools and established relationships are always significant, but too often ignored. Together with evidence about the limits of school improvement based on individual schools, this study suggests that a national education system raising standards for all students, in all schools, requires the systematic and locally organized redistribution of available resources and expertise through a contextually sensitive collaboration strategy.

BEYOND THE SCHOOL GATES: CONTEXT, DISADVANTAGE AND 'URBAN SCHOOLS'

Alan Dyson

While most of the chapters in this book are focused on the removal of barriers to progress within urban schools, there are other equally significant barriers that are located in the wider contexts in which schools work. This chapter considers the implication of these external factors for school improvement efforts. In so doing it questions whether schools alone can overcome the disadvantages that arise from economic poverty. The author argues that new forms of leadership are needed which recognize the contexts within which schools operate, both in terms of the social and economic contexts that envelop their students, and of the wider policy and practice contexts which are relevant to overcoming disadvantage.

A couple of years ago, colleagues and I undertook a study of the role that schools in urban contexts might play in area regeneration (Crowther et al. 2003). Since there was little evidence that schools actually were contributing to regeneration initiatives in any explicit way, much of the study focused on how school leaders understood the communities they served and what they thought their relationship with these communities should be.

In the course of the study, I interviewed two urban comprehensive school headteachers in the same local education authority area. Their schools were remarkably similar in terms of size, population and levels of attainment. They were located about a mile and a half apart, on either side of the social housing estate which was the focus of our study, and drew their intakes from that estate and other equally disadvantaged areas nearby.

When I asked them how they viewed the role of their schools vis-à-vis these disadvantaged communities, they were both equally clear, but diametrically opposed in their views. The head of 'Shepherd' Comprehensive told me, in no uncertain terms, that local communities were dysfunctional and that they were the principal reason why his school's students struggled to achieve. Far from developing links with local communities, his job, he said, was to turn the school into a very different sort of community which would insulate students from the pernicious influences beyond the school gate.

The head of 'Bellamy' Comprehensive, by contrast, was clear that the school stood little chance of raising students' attainments unless it developed strong, positive relationships with local communities. Family members and local residents had to become involved with the school and engaged in learning if a community culture was to be created within which children and young people could themselves come to value learning. This was, however, a task that was too big for one school acting alone. Accordingly, he was leading a group of local schools in a proposal to establish an Education Action Zone (EAZ) which would focus on developing school–community relations.

These very different views of what urban schools are and how they should relate to local communities raise important issues. How does a school in a disadvantaged urban context raise the achievements of its students – and why are those achievements almost invariably low in the first place? What is the proper role for an urban school? Is it purely an educational institution or does it have wider responsibilities to the disadvantaged families and communities it serves? And what does it mean to lead schools such as these? Is it about creating a learning-oriented counter culture through the actions of high quality, well-organized teachers? Or is it about some wider notion of community action in which the school leader is simply one of a number of professionals and community members trying somehow to make a difference to a disadvantaged area?

The story of the two heads has a significant coda. As the second, community-oriented head was finalizing his EAZ proposal, the Department for Education and Skills (DfES) shifted its ground in terms of what it was prepared to fund. Whereas previously it had encouraged innovation and local initiative, the apparent lack of any impact on attainments in disadvantaged areas led it to take tighter control and insist that proposals should be much more explicitly attainment focused. The EAZ was funded, therefore, but most of its community strands had to be jettisoned. It also became clear that the head was out of step with an LEA which followed very closely the government's lead and offered little encouragement to initiatives that were not clearly focused on 'standards'. Before the end of our study, the head resigned at short notice under what seemed to us to be something of a cloud.

Whatever else was going on here, it is clear that national policy played a great part in shaping what could or could not be done at school level. In this chapter, therefore, I shall attempt to address some of the questions raised by the case of these two headteachers and, particularly, to do so by considering how national policy has, explicitly or implicitly, answered these questions. Finally, I shall return to the question of what it means to lead a school serving disadvantaged urban contexts.

'Urban schools' and disadvantage

I described the two schools above as being in some sense 'urban'. The concepts of 'the urban' and of 'urban schools' are, however, problematic.

Frequently, 'urban' is used as a shorthand for 'disadvantaged' and 'urban schools' are seen stereotypically as those which serve highly disadvantaged inner-city areas or large suburban social housing estates. When, in the early 1990s, Ofsted produced a report (Ofsted 1993) that was highly critical of urban schools – and that effectively launched a wave of concern that continues to the present – it seems to have been these stereotypically urban schools that they had in mind.

There are two reasons for being cautious about this stereotype. The first is that it is simply inaccurate. While there are indeed many 'urban' schools which serve highly disadvantaged areas and where educational attainments are low, there are many others which are not like this. Most major towns and cities contain relatively affluent areas where families send their children to much more favoured schools, or, indeed, to fee-paying independent schools and, beyond this, there is usually a local hierarchy of schools from the most favoured to the most disadvantaged. Moreover, even those schools with highly disadvantaged populations differ from each other: some serve multi-ethnic populations, some are almost exclusively mono-ethnic; some recruit from a small area around the school, some have a much more dispersed catchment; some are located close to areas of considerable wealth and opportunity while others serve populations that are marooned in disadvantage; some, it would appear, are succeeding 'against the odds' while others appear to be sinking fast. For all of these reasons, it is sometimes helpful to think in terms of 'schools in (very different) urban contexts' rather than of stereotypically 'urban schools'.

The second reason for being cautious about the stereotype is that schools with highly disadvantaged populations are simply particular examples of a much wider phenomenon. That phenomenon is the so-called 'cycle of disadvantage' whereby a disadvantaged social background increases the risk of low educational achievement and low achievement tends to limit subsequent life chances. It is arguable that this phenomenon is particularly acute and visible in schools in some urban contexts, but, of course, by no means all people living in disadvantage also live in major towns and cities and by no means all their children attend stereotypically urban schools. However, it has been convenient for successive governments to highlight these extreme examples because the 'problem' can then be located in the supposed malfunctions of a limited number of institutions rather than in the more deeply structural production and reproduction of disadvantage. This is an issue to which we shall return shortly.

As with the stereotype of 'urban schools', the focus on particular schools contains a half-truth which it is important to unpack. We know that disadvantage is reproduced in complex ways, but education is an important mediating factor between the disadvantage experienced by the family and the life chances of the family's children. Not only does education impact on young people's life chances directly, but it also has a role to play in family processes which themselves impact on children's capacities and outcomes (Feinstein et al. 2004). In principle, therefore, the education system – largely, though not exclusively, in the form of statutory schooling – offers a means whereby the state can intervene in the reproduction of disadvantage so as to equalize life chances between individuals from different social backgrounds (de Carvalho 2001).

In this country, this equity agenda has been evident for many years – in the creation of grammar schools to offer opportunities to 'able' working-class children, for instance and in the subsequent spread of comprehensive schools as a more effective engine for equalizing educational outcomes and life chances (Benn and Simon 1972). I take it that it is also evident in the multiple initiatives directed at urban schools by New Labour governments since 1997 – and I shall have more to say of these later. However, it is clear that, despite successive waves of reform, Basil Bernstein's dictum that 'education cannot compensate for society' (Bernstein 1970) remains more or less as true today as it was at the start of the 1970s. A recent report from the Centre for Economic Performance (Blanden et al. 2005), for instance, finds that intergenerational mobility (that is, the ability of people to achieve a socioeconomic status different from that of their birth family) in England is low compared with most other economically rich countries; far from increasing, there is evidence that mobility was less for people born in the 1970 cohort than for those born in 1958, with mixed outcomes for later cohorts; and a major factor in limiting mobility is the strong relationship between family income and educational attainment – with children from better-off families taking greatest advantage of any new educational opportunities that may arise.

The widespread nature of this phenomenon suggests that it cannot be attributed to the problems of a limited number of 'urban' schools. Nonetheless, there is some evidence that the spatial concentration of disadvantage in some urban contexts strengthens the links between disadvantage, attainment and life chances. In recent years, for instance, as standards of measured educational attainment rise nationally, it is the most disadvantaged areas which make least progress, thus increasing the gap between them and their more advantaged counterparts (Machin et al. 2005). The focus on schools in such areas, therefore, is not entirely misguided. However, as I argued earlier, if such schools are a special case, they are a special case which illustrates in acute form a much wider phenomenon.

Policy interventions in urban schools

In this situation, it is not surprising that successive governments have attempted in various ways to intervene in the poverty–attainment–life-chance relationship and that some of their efforts have focused on the 'special case' of schools serving highly disadvantaged urban contexts. All such interventions, of course, rest upon some more or less explicit theory about how, precisely, social background produces effects on educational attainment and how, in turn, attainments impact on life chances. Rothstein (2004), for instance, proposes three theoretical understandings that have found favour at various times and places: a genetic understanding, which proposes that people are poor and attain poorly because they are genetically inferior to their peers; a health conceptualization, which proposes that poor children do badly at school because they are prone to ill-health; and a sociocultural understanding, which proposes that the cultures and identities of poor groups are different from those of dominant school cultures and lead to their disengagement and failure in the school context.

There are undoubtedly other theories that might be and have been advanced. If, for instance, we focus on the policy interventions which have been made in recent years – particularly under New Labour governments – we can detect a somewhat different account. Some aspects of New Labour's education policy – and of the ideology which underpins it – have been discussed extensively in the literature. It is well understood, for instance, that there has been a focus on standards, the reform of educational structures and practices, the continuing marketization of the education system and the creation of a culture of performativity (Phillips and Harper-Jones 2003: 126). However, there is sometimes less recognition that New Labour policy has also been characterized by a determined effort to intervene in the disadvantage–attainment–life-chance relationship or that this effort has been underpinned by a more or less explicit theory about how this relationship works.

This theory is encapsulated most clearly in its use of a concept of 'social exclusion', defined by the Prime Minister in the following terms:

> Social exclusion is a shorthand label for what can happen when individuals or areas suffer from a combination of linked problems such as unemployment, poor skills, low incomes, poor housing, high crime environments, bad health and family breakdown. The Government have policies that are targeted at reducing all of these individually, but Government programmes have been less good at tackling the interaction between these problems or preventing them from arising in the first place.
>
> The purpose of the unit is to help break this vicious circle and coordinate and improve Government action to reduce social exclusion
>
> (Blair 1997a)

Blair also argued that, after a lengthy period of Conservative government, people need to be given back their 'will to win':

> For 18 years, the poorest people in our country have been forgotten by government. They have been left out of growing prosperity, told that they were not needed, ignored by the Government except for the purpose of blaming them. I want that to change. There will be no forgotten people in the Britain I want to build.
>
> We need to act in a new way because fatalism, and not just poverty, is the problem we face, the dead weight of low expectations, the crushing belief that things cannot get better. I want to give people back the will to win again.
>
> (Blair 1997b)

This is an interesting analysis of the way in which disadvantage is produced and reproduced in society. What is most striking is that there is no sense here of either a genetic or structural determinism. In other words, people are not disadvantaged because in some sense they are incapable of doing better, nor are they held back by the insuperable barriers created by social structures.

Barriers there most certainly are, but they arise from government neglect and, the implication is, can be overcome by concerted government action which will release people's inherent energies and enable them to make their own way to better things.

In this context the role of education is vital. It is not for nothing that Blair famously described his three priorities as 'education, education and education'. In the absence of insuperable barriers to well-being, education becomes a principal determinant of how individuals and groups will fare socially. As Blair explained:

> Why are we so keen to raise standards in our schools? Because the quickest route to the workless class is to fail your English and maths class. In today's world, the more you learn, the more you earn.
>
> (Blair 1997b)

The focus on standards, modernization, choice and diversity and performativity, therefore, are means to fundamental social ends. Put simply, if the education system can be made more effective, if in particular 'standards' can be driven up in those parts of the system serving disadvantaged groups and if this educational improvement can be accompanied by other policies to address the range of barriers experienced by these groups, then there is no reason why disadvantage should not be overcome. As the DfES School Improvement and Excellence Team puts it:

> Our aim is to transform the delivery of education so that every pupil has the opportunity to reach his or her true potential.
>
> (DfES no date)

Indeed, the range of initiatives for which this team is responsible – Excellence in Cities, Schools Facing Challenging Circumstances, Leadership Incentive Grant and the like – typifies much in the government's approach to education and disadvantage. In the absence of structural barriers and given the key role of education, the focus has been on the functioning of schools generally, with extra attention paid to those serving disadvantaged areas. These schools have been targeted with extra resources and support, they have been subject to incentives and penalties and their leaders have been given autonomy, encouragement and training on the assumption that, at some point, they will be able to make the breakthrough with their students. These previously disengaged, underachieving children and young people will, under the right circumstances, begin to switch on to learning, rediscover their 'will to win' and go forward to a brighter future.

Emerging problems

There is no doubt that this view of the role of education in relation to disadvantage has proved immensely energizing, not least to education professionals working in what were previously seen as hopeless situations. There are also, as we see in the chapters of this book, success stories to tell – the initial hike in primary attainment scores, for instance, some indications of the lowest performing schools doing better at GCSE level and multiple accounts of such schools being 'turned round' by energetic and charismatic head-teachers. However, as I suggested earlier, evidence that the historical links between disadvantage, low educational achievement and limited life chances have been definitively broken is hard to come by. Indeed, a recent review of New Labour's overall anti-poverty strategy suggests that, not only are out-comes in education mixed, but that this matches a somewhat patchy and ambiguous picture across the whole range of policy (Hills and Stewart 2005). At the very least, it is not clear whether such gains as there have been indicate a real break in the 'cycle of disadvantage' or whether they represent simply a series of rather 'soft' gains that leave the underlying relationship undisturbed.

In terms of practice, the problems with the New Labour approach have become increasingly apparent as time has gone on. Some time ago, Gillborn and Youdell reported on the process of educational 'triage' whereby schools focused on those students most likely to help them hit their targets and selected out students least likely to make progress (Gillborn and Youdell 2000). Since then there has been a growing acknowledgement – even in official circles (see, for instance, Statistics Commission 2005) – that such apparent gains as there have been are far from deeply embedded and may simply be the consequence of schools' learning how to teach to the test and how to engage in strategic behaviour in chasing their targets.

In fact there are a number of problematic issues in the current situation. First, if, as some have suggested (Tymms 2001, 2004) the apparent gains from the New Labour approach are largely or partially illusory, then they are unlikely to represent the hoped-for break in the link between disadvantage and low achievement. Second, if schools are indeed engaging in strategic behaviour to reach their targets, then it may well be that the best interests of their students – or at least of some of their students – are being scarified on the altar of institutional advantage. Third, if schools are busily chasing targets, they may be neglecting some more fundamental reforms which may be needed before the disadvantage–low achievement link can really be tackled.

The problems with the overall approach – and the dilemmas facing schools – are neatly illustrated in an initiative which colleagues and I are currently evaluating. The initiative is aimed at making a difference to education in parts of a northern city ('Northtown') where standards have historically been low and where there are multiple social problems. In a style now familiar from Education Action Zones and Excellence in Cities initiatives, participating schools have been targeted with extra funding, have been offered broad – but certainly not prescriptive – guidance on how to spend it. They have been encouraged to use their own judgement in setting up schemes and forms of provision which meet what they understand to be the needs of their students. Again, in a manner which is typical of recent policy initiatives, schools have been set performance targets which they have to attain. In this case, the initiative is making use of Neighbourhood Renewal Fund (NRF) money, so schools have been required to help meet the 'floor targets' for performance that are common to Neighbourhood Renewal areas. In order to do so, schools have been encouraged to focus their attentions on students who are on the borderline of the target levels of achievement.

The results have been predictable. Schools have identified a handful of students who they feel are capable of reaching the required levels but are currently unlikely to do so. A familiar array of strategies has then appeared to help these students over the borderline – extra tuition, mentoring, rewards for effort, motivational tutoring, Saturday schools and the like. Needless to say, some at least of the students have obliged by performing better than expected in tests and the schools are delighted that they seem to be making good progress towards their targets.

However, the doubts about an initiative such as this are manifold. What prospect is there that gains from hot-housing of this kind are likely to be sustainable? What happens to the other students who are not targeted? What happens when the additional funding runs out? What happens when students move to their next school or into post-16 provision and find they are no longer targeted for special attention? Questions such as these are already familiar from other studies of schools serving disadvantaged areas which have adopted instrumental approaches to improvement (see Reynolds et al. 2001 for an overview).

Ironically, it is clear that the schools themselves have some sense that something more is needed. In addition to targeting and coaching, they are also developing a range of more broadly based strategies: in some, the mentoring is focused on personal development and engagement with learning rather than simply on test-passing; in others, there are experiments with a more flexible curriculum aimed at giving students the opportunity to achieve in areas other than literacy and numeracy; secondary schools are developing opportunities for work-based and vocational learning; and some of the schools are involved in schemes which give local people employment on the school site.

None of these approaches is without its problems. However, they all signal an emerging understanding that an instrumental focus on targets and attainment are unlikely to work in the highly problematic context of schools serving disadvantaged areas – at least not if that is all that is on offer. At a recent workshop, the participating heads and teachers began to talk about this alternative approach in terms of, 'making schools the way they ought to be', by which they meant, making them more welcoming and more engaging for children and young people who currently find them alienating and hostile. However, this alternative approach remains embryonic: the pressure from the local authority to target and achieve remains relentless; there is no means whereby schools can work together to develop their 'alternative' approaches; and the interventions of different schools remain almost entirely disconnected from each other.

Towards an alternative

What the Northtown experience points to is the realization within many schools that centrally prescribed teaching techniques, 'effective' teachers and dynamic school leadership alone may not be enough to engage students in learning. A more holistic approach which acknowledges questions of learner identity, cultural expectations and the nature of teacher–learner relationships may also be needed. In this respect, the Northtown schools follow closely the pattern set by other schools with which colleagues and myself have worked where this more holistic approach, characterized as 'inclusive', came to be seen as an essential accompaniment and counterweight to the dominant orthodoxy of standards (Ainscow et al. in press). A reasonable hypothesis seems to be that teachers, facing the reality of children and young people on a daily basis, have no alternative but to shape their approaches in response to those realities – in ways which policymakers are apt to overlook.

However, even these more holistic and responsive approaches fail to overcome the limits of the dominant response to disadvantage embodied in national policy. The issue may not be that current government policies have failed to raise the performance of schools sufficiently far, nor even that there may be different forms of practice in schools which could achieve better results, but, that the school may be the wrong place to start in tackling the disadvantage–attainment–life-chance relationship. It makes sense to begin with the school so long as it can be assumed that the impact of schooling is, in principle, sufficiently powerful to overcome the effects of disadvantage. However, the evidence for this assumption is dubious, to say the least.

As we saw earlier, despite well over a century of state schooling and successive attempts to reform the system in ways which will make outcomes more equal, attainment continues to be very strongly correlated with social background. There must be, at the very least, strong doubts as to whether *any* form of schooling is going to prove powerful enough to change this relationship. Moreover, there is increasing evidence that the impact of schools on relative levels of student attainment is limited. Estimates vary, but it seems that the school level factors account for only about 10 percent of the variance in attainment, with the remainder being accounted for by teacher effects and even more by the psychological characteristics of students and their social backgrounds (Mortimore and Whitty 2000; Teddlie and Reynolds 2000). While it remains theoretically possible that some yet to be discovered form of schooling might indeed be powerful enough to make the school a major determiner of learning, the implication is that making all schools as 'effective' as the best will not in itself do much to overcome the effects of disadvantage.

Furthermore, there are doubts as to whether the aim of making all schools equally 'effective' is realistic. Studies of the impact of context on school processes suggests that schools serving disadvantaged populations may find it more difficult than others to 'improve' in the sense of generating higher attainments (Thrupp 1999; Lupton 2004a, b). Far from schools overcoming the effects of disadvantage, it seems more likely that those effects reach into the school and constrain the processes through which it seeks to drive up attainments. Not surprisingly, therefore, even where schools serving disadvantaged areas do generate some improvements, it is evident that those improvements are fragile and may depend on changes in the surrounding area rather than on the quality of the school (Maden 2001). Moreover, as we saw earlier, the evidence of recent school reforms in England seems to be that any improvements in schools serving disadvantaged areas are at least matched if not outshone by those of their more advantaged counterparts.

Although, therefore, the system as a whole may 'improve', this does nothing to change the *relative* low achievement of those from disadvantaged circumstances.

These considerations create something of a contradiction in current education policy and in more general efforts at school improvement. A DfES commissioned study of schools serving highly disadvantaged former coalfield areas, for instance, concludes that:

- The dominant factors affecting school performance in the former coalfield areas are those associated with extreme social disadvantage. These negative external factors are compounded in certain coalfield areas and present a significant challenge to schools in raising levels of achievement.
- In order to raise achievement and to sustain levels of achievement in the former coalfield areas patterns of socio-economic disadvantage have to be recognised and, where possible, addressed. The difficulties facing the schools are not independent from the problems facing the wider community.

(Harris et al. 2003: 1)

However, the bulk of the report is concerned not with strategies for addressing these factors beyond the school gate, but with rehearsing a familiar litany of school improvement measures – distributed leadership, high expectations, positive relationships and the like, which sit well with the dominant thrust of national policy but do nothing to address the underlying disadvantage which does most to explain the low attainments in these schools.

The issue here is not that New Labour governments have been unable to formulate policy interventions to deal with disadvantage beyond the school gates. On the contrary, there have been, for instance, the Child Poverty strategy and the Neighbourhood Renewal strategy which have been centrally concerned with overcoming the effects of family and area disadvantage. However, despite the Prime Minister's determination in 1997 to see social exclusion tackled in a coordinated way, non-educational and educational interventions have been largely driven in parallel rather than as a coherent whole. There has, therefore, been no requirement for schools to contribute to wider anti-disadvantage strategies or even to consider the implications of their actions for those strategies. Some school leaders, like the headteacher of Bellamy Comprehensive have nonetheless begun to explore a wider role. Others, however, like his counterpart at Shepherd Comprehensive have cut themselves off from wider considerations and pursued their own agendas. Many, like the Northfield schools, have sensed that there is a wider task to undertake but have been encouraged and cajoled to focus on a narrow agenda of test-passing and target-meeting, regardless of how this impacts on wider strategies. Ironically, in Northtown this is the case despite the fact that the initiative is funded by the Neighbourhood Renewal Fund.

There have, of course, been some potentially important recent changes. The *Every Child Matters* agenda, operationalized in the Children Act 2004 and supported by a range of guidance documents (DfES 2003a, 2004a, b, c), promises to take a holistic view of the needs of children and families and to create integrated structures and services aimed at meeting those needs in a coherent and coordinated way. At the same time, the development of Extended and Full-Service Extended Schools (DfES 2002, 2003b, no date), offering a range of services to children, families and communities and acting as the base for other community agencies seems to offer a new model of schooling which will be much less narrowly focused than its immediate predecessors.

Colleagues and I have been involved in evaluating the latter set of initiatives (Dyson et al. 2002; Cummings et al. 2004, 2005) and there are indeed signs of things beginning to be done differently. Some schools have set up an impressive array of activities and services for children, their families and communities. They have developed, in some cases, a sense of how their work with these three constituencies interacts. Typically, they claim that they are aiming to change attitudes towards learning and wider cultures of aspiration and achievement in families and communities as a means of changing attitudes and levels of achievement among their students. Like the Northtown schools, they recognize that a unidimensional focus on 'standards' is not in itself able to impact sufficiently. Unlike them, however, they have systems and strategies for addressing wider issues. Indeed, in some cases, the work of these schools is set within the context of local strategies for the regeneration of neighbourhoods or even whole towns which align their work with policies in housing, economic development, crime reduction and community development. Where this is the case, schools commonly work not as isolated educational institutions, but as part of a network of other schools and community agencies supporting each other and pooling their resources in a sustained effort to address disadvantage in the areas they serve.

In many ways, these schools share the vision of the head of Bellamy Comprehensive – though, unlike him, they have the means and support to participate in a wide-ranging community strategy. However, it is important not to romanticize their work. First, despite some promising short-term and small-scale outcomes, there is no evidence that approaches such as these are capable of having a significant impact on achievement such that we can say with any confidence that they are likely to change the relationship of low achievement to disadvantage (Sammons et al. 2003; Wilkin et al. 2003; Cummings et al. 2005). Second – and not unconnected with this – the changes in approach which they embody are actually rather superficial. Although services are reconfigured and relocated, there is little if any new money and arguably no new services. Despite the promising developments in some places, the focus of most activities is on offering individual children, young people and adults various forms of support rather than on structural changes in the social or economic contexts which generate so many of their problems in the first place. By and large, schools continue to subscribe to the government orthodoxy that education is the principal solution to disadvantage and to see their 'full-service' provision primarily as a means of ensuring that the 'barriers to learning' created for students by their dysfunctional environments are removed.

It may be that developments such as these simply need time so that they can grow in scope and power. However, it may also be that a more radical – in the sense of a more fundamentally oriented – approach is needed. Lloyd and Payne (2003), for instance, argue that progressive education reform aimed at reducing disadvantage is possible, but that it needs to be set in the context of new economic and social models which are themselves less divisive and unequal. It is possible, therefore, that changes in schooling such as those I have described can be used simply to mask the worst effects of structural inequalities as, some would argue, has been the case in the USA (see, for instance, Moss et al. 1999). On the other hand, there remains the possibility that such changes could accompany and interact with wider social and economic changes which would give them new power and new meaning.

Coda: reflections on leadership

The issue of school leadership has been implicit rather than explicit throughout most of this chapter – and that is deliberate. The foregrounding of leadership issues in recent years, both in policy and in research, is of a piece with New Labour's view of the central role of education and the nature of social exclusion. It rests on the assumption that school leaders have real freedom of action – not in the sense that they are freed from legislative and governance constraints, where that freedom has arguably decreased, but in the sense that they are not constrained by the nature of their school populations and the role ascribed to schools by national policies and their underpinning ideologies. Likewise, it assumes that their actions make a difference, that they can create 'effective' schools and that such schools are capable of changing the disadvantage–achievement relationship. It will be clear from all that I have said in this chapter that I reject these assumptions. School leadership is important, but it is not the place where the battle against disadvantage will be won.

Amidst all the current talk, therefore, of effective leadership, assertive leadership and, latterly, of 'distributed' leadership, I wish to argue for something that might be called 'contextualized' leadership. This is leadership which recognizes the contexts within which schools operate, both in terms of the social and economic contexts which envelop their students and of the wider policy and practice contexts which are relevant to overcoming disadvantage. In particular, it redefines the responsibilities of school leaders, not in terms of the concerns and advantages of the individual institution, but of a wider social strategy within which the institution is one agent among many. Some of the practical characteristics of contextualized leadership are evident in the heads of some Full-Service Extended Schools and, indeed, in the community-oriented head whose case opened this chapter. They include:

- a recognition of the important but limited role which schooling plays in overcoming disadvantage;
- a willingness to participate in local strategies and work alongside other educationalists and non-educationalists within a network of provision;

- a readiness to think in terms broader than targets, measured attainments and institutional advantage;
- an understanding of the social and economic contexts of children, families and communities and of the role of other agencies within those contexts;
- an ability to lead the school not only in driving up attainment but in making connections with children and families cultures and expectations.

Such headteachers undoubtedly already exist in reality and there are many more who might potentially work in this way. However, national policy has hitherto made it difficult for them to thrive (as in our first example) and it is still not clear that recent changes will make things substantially easier. The recent drive from the National College for School leadership towards developing 'community leadership' may signal an important rethinking of the way leadership is understood at policy level. However, it may also simply mean that unreconstructed school leaders, whose priorities lie in 'standards' and institutional advantage, are encouraged to marshal families and communities in support of those priorities. What is needed, therefore, is not simply a re-skilling of school leaders, but a new policy framework within which those new skills can be allowed to flourish.

12

DRAWING OUT THE LESSONS: LEADERSHIP AND COLLABORATION

Mel Ainscow and Mel West

This final chapter reflects on the accounts presented in previous chapters. It argues that the findings of the research reported point to important new possibilities for improving the quality of education in urban contexts. Given that there is untapped potential within the system, it is proposed that our aim must be to develop leadership practices that encourage collaboration within and between schools, so that individual knowledge, experience and creativity can be shared for the benefit of all. It is also argued that such collaborations have to reach out to the wider community. The chapter goes on to examine the implications of these arguments for policy development, and considers their significance at the national, district and institutional levels.

The accounts presented in this book provide interesting insights into some of the pressures on and developments within urban educational contexts in England during a period of extraordinary change. Our analysis of these accounts leads us to conclude that significant advances in urban schooling are unlikely to be achieved unless those who remain on the margins of the system are transformed into full participants. However, as we have seen, external efforts to raise standards in poorly performing schools often create barriers to the development of a more inclusive approach.

The government has argued that the raising of 'standards' must also promote equity: that a powerful emphasis on raising attainment need not simply benefit children who are already performing at a high level. Implemented properly, and supported by the various inclusion initiatives, the standards agenda is, it is argued, of even greater potential benefit to previously low-attaining children in poorly performing schools: it is about excellence for the many, not just the few.

Yet the national strategies, whatever their benefits, have tended to reduce the flexibility with which schools can respond to the diverse characteristics of their students. As the accounts of what happens inside schools that are deemed to be 'failing' (reported in Chapters 2, 3 and 4) demonstrate, this has been a particular problem for those urban schools that are seen to be performing poorly, since the short-term pressure to deliver satisfactory 'metrics' can postpone the development of strategies necessary for longer term improvement. And, as is evident from the study of schools that have made sustained progress, despite the drag-anchor of being identified as 'below floor targets' (reported in Chapter 5), headteachers are acutely aware of such pressures.

While the need to escape such designations can be useful in galvanizing early efforts, since the designation itself becomes a common enemy upon which energies can be focused, they may also be limiting and inhibit ambition – among students and teachers alike. At the same time, the development during the 1990s of an educational market-place, coupled with the recent emphasis on policies fostering greater diversity between schools, seems in some areas to have created a quasi-selective system in which the poorest children, by and large, attend the lowest performing schools. Consequently the lowest performing and, many would argue, the least advantaged schools fall progressively further and further behind their high-performing counterparts. In terms of these effects, through selective advantaging and disadvantaging of schools, it can be argued that those very policies that have generally led to increased standards, have also increased, rather than decreased, disparities in education quality and opportunity between advantaged and less privileged groups. Giroux and Schmidt (2004) explain how similar reform policies in the United States have turned some schools into 'test-prep centres'. As a result, such schools tend to be increasingly ruthless in their disregard of those students who pose a threat to their 'success', as determined by standardized but narrow assessment procedures.

Nevertheless, our analysis of the experiences described in this book also offers some reasons for optimism, not least in that it suggests that the system has considerable untapped potential to improve itself. As we have seen, there are skills, knowledge and, most importantly, creativity within schools, and within their local communities, that can be mobilized to improve educational provision. We have seen examples of how school staff groups can come together to strengthen and increase the impact of one another's efforts (Chapters 2, 3, 5 and 6); we have seen the impact of headteachers pooling their knowledge and experience for the benefit of a particular school (Chapter 8) or for a group of schools (Chapters 9 and 10); we have seen the potential for cooperation between schools and their local authority (Chapter 7) and with the wider community (Chapters 5 and 11); and, running throughout all the chapters, we have also seen the potential of partnerships between school staff and researchers.

All of this demonstrates what can be achieved when those who have a stake in urban education engage in authentic collaborative activity. Of course, collaboration has itself been a regular feature of national policy in recent years, best illustrated by Excellence in Cities and the Leadership Incentive Grant (LIG), both initiatives specifically targeted at schools in challenging urban environments. Nevertheless, and despite this press for greater collaboration within and between schools, there has been a tendency to view urban schools through a deficit lens, focusing on what they lack rather than on the resources on which they can draw. As a result, it has often been assumed that externally driven strategies are the only feasible means of achieving improvement. While our own recent work with LIG collaboratives (Ainscow et al. 2005) leaves us in no doubt about the importance of additional resources as a stimulus for school to school collaboration, we are also aware of the potency of local ownership and local ideas. Our experiences suggest that national improvement strategies have, too often, fallen into the trap of overlooking the evidence that local interpretation and adaptation can shape and strengthen the way proposals are implemented. Indeed, it seems to us that this helps to explain why these initiatives have had rather mixed effects. Dyson's description of 'Northtown' schools (Chapter 11) provides an excellent illustration of both how the local element can and must contribute, and how national policies can discourage such contributions.

Of course, the pressures arising from inspection and from the publishing of Ofsted reports and test and examination results have certainly focused minds. In some instances, this has also inspired a degree of rethinking and experimentation. But, as Chapters 2, 3 and 4 make clear, it has sometimes encouraged staff to take a rather insular approach – after all, what one school 'contributes' to the success of another does not appear in any league table. At the same time, the political imperative to achieve rapid results, particularly the desire to identify strategies that 'work' and then to 'up-scale' these through centrally determined prescriptions, has created barriers to progress. Further, the tendency to designate some schools as failing, or causing concern, can place restrictions on the willingness of those involved to take risks. Again, Chapter 11 provides us with a pertinent example here – 'Shepherd' Comprehensive, opted to exclude the local community and establish, instead, some sort of educational oasis, where national policies (and the values implicit in these) were imposed even more strongly to eliminate the (presumably malign) influences of the local environment. It avoided the risks of opening up the school to the community, and instead pursued strategies that required changes in the community, rather than changes in the way we think about the business of schools, in order to achieve sustainable success.

However, we remain optimistic that schools can find ways to work together and with their communities that will enable some of the disadvantages of location and catchment to be overcome. The remainder of this chapter sets out what we feel is needed if this is to happen. It is organized around what we see as the major themes arising from the accounts we have gathered together here. These are the need to think more deeply about what collaboration means; the importance of leadership within collaboration and the pressures collaboration places on school leaders; strategies and practices that can promote collaborative activity; and the importance of identifying and using the skills and imagination of existing staff, since there is no alternative teaching force 'out there' that, if we could only attract them, will come in and transform our more challenging schools. Finally, we focus on what emerges from these studies as a key issue – knowing how to get things moving.

Understanding collaboration

The development of collaboration as a strategy for school improvement is far from straightforward within the English context where competition and choice continue to be driving forces within national education policy. This is why powerful levers are needed that will challenge existing assumptions and, at the same time, move thinking and practice forward. However, we feel that there is also a need to explicate what it is collaboration brings that adds value to school improvement efforts.

Our own understanding of the potential of collaborative working practices has been shaped, in part, by the projects reported in this book. It has also been influenced by the ideas of Wenger (1998), Senge (1990) and Hargreaves (2003). Wenger, in putting forward his notion of 'communities of practice', describes the transfer and creation of knowledge within the workplace. Essentially, the members of a work community pass on their knowledge and ideas to one another through processes of 'negotiation' in which common meanings are established. 'New' knowledge acquired in this way can then be tested out in practice – though inevitably it will be modified as it is subjected to new experiences and contexts. As it moves around within the community, passing from practitioner to practitioner, knowledge is continually modified and refined. In this way, it becomes possible for knowledge to be recycled around the community and returned to the originator – though transformed through the process. Thus, the virtuous circle is completed, with knowledge and understanding increased through each iteration.

Senge, in his writings on learning organizations, suggests that knowledge within organizations takes two forms – the explicit and the tacit. Explicit knowledge (which will embrace established wisdom), is relatively easy to transfer, but is likely to be generalized rather than specific. On the other hand, tacit knowledge is caught rather than deliberately passed on, but can only be caught if the right circumstances exist. Consequently, what can be achieved through explicit and tacit exchanges is limited – learning organizations need to find ways to generate tacit to explicit and explicit to tacit transfers. Again, our conception of collaborative practice is that it provides just such an opportunity, as individuals work together on common goals, sharing and using one another's knowledge and, through the processes of sharing, reflection and recycling, create new knowledge.

David Hargreaves also notes the tacit nature of much of teachers' knowledge when explaining why it has proved so difficult to transfer good practice from one teacher to another. This leads him to conclude that what he describes as 'social capital' is needed within the teaching communities. Social capital here represents shared values and assumptions that, because they are commonly 'owned' by community members, are available for all members of the community to draw on when transferring knowledge and understandings. For him, building social capital involves the development of networks based on mutual trust, within which good practice can spread in natural ways.

Bearing these ideas in mind, we suggest that collaboration within and between schools is a practice that can both transfer existing knowledge and, more importantly, generate context-specific 'new' knowledge. Further, we feel that the studies reported in this book give strong indications of how such processes can be initiated and managed. At the same time, these experiences also point to certain conditions that are necessary in order to make collaboration effective. In summary, these are as follows:

- The presence of incentives that encourage key stakeholders to explore the possibility that collaboration will be in their own interests;
- The development of a sense of collective responsibility for bringing about improvements in all the partner organizations;
- Headteachers and other senior staff in schools who are willing and able to drive collaboration forward;
- The identification of common improvement priorities that are seen to be relevant to a wide range of stakeholders;
- External help from credible consultants/advisers (from the local authority or elsewhere) who also have the disposition and confidence to learn alongside their school-based partners; and
- A willingness and desire among local authority staff to support and engage with the collaborative process, exploring and developing new roles and relationships.

In our view, the absence of such conditions will mean that attempts to encourage teachers and schools to work together are likely to result in little more than time consuming meetings, which sooner or later will be seen as ineffective and be discontinued. This conclusion is, in itself, important for future national initiatives that seek to invest resources in the notion of schools working together in partnerships or networks. Strategies for developing these conditions – or fostering their development at the local level – will be an important determinant of the success such initiatives can expect. This analysis also suggests that the government's current emphasis on the spread of 'independent specialist schools' and academies needs to be handled sensitively, if it is not to further disadvantage schools and groups of learners that are already struggling against the odds.

Leadership for collaboration

We now turn to another theme emerging from our analysis of these studies – leadership. However, we would like to emphasize that while it is true that, by and large, schools do not improve without effective leadership from the inside, it is also the case that the wider context influences the progress of such improvement efforts, for good or ill. This is the power of what is characterized in Chapter 7 as 'interdependence'. It leads us to argue that, while in order to secure sustained improvement, schools do have to become more autonomous and self-improving, at the same time, our attention should not be drawn away from the ways that neighbouring schools can add value to one another's efforts.

The research summarized in this book has led us to formulate a typology of the sorts of relationships that can exist within a network of schools. Where the individual school locates itself within the typology is a critical factor in determining whether or not collaborative arrangements bring benefits, and the attitude of the headteacher appears to be a crucial determinant of positioning. The typology, which draws on the ideas of Michael Fielding (1999), postulates four levels of collaborative endeavour, as follows:

- *Association*: This is the traditional pattern, where there are some links between schools through occasional LEA meetings and in-service events. By and large, however, it does not involve sharing of knowledge or resources.
- *Cooperation*: This is where closer links develop through participation in meetings and activities that provide opportunities to contribute experiences. As a result there may be some incidental sharing of knowledge and resources, and thus some transfer of existing knowledge.
- *Collaboration*: This involves schools working together to address particular problems or challenges. By their nature, such activities require the sharing of knowledge and resources, but often these initiatives are focused on specific objectives and are not sustained. However, there are limited opportunities for knowledge creation, though recycling is less common, as such collaboration most often assumes 'stronger' and 'weaker' partners.
- *Collegiality*: This involves a wider and longer term relationship, between schools and teachers, in which there is recognition of interdependence and, to a degree, the sharing of responsibility for one another's progress. It leads to the bringing together of existing knowledge and resources within an agreed set of values and, potentially, the creation of new knowledge for all. In this way, collegiality provides a network within which social capital can be built up.

Such a typology suggests that the aim must be to foster moves towards the more powerful, interdependent, collaborative relationships that can strengthen the capacity of all partner schools to deliver forms of education that can respond effectively to student diversity. In this regard, the distinction made by Fielding between 'collaboration' and 'collegiality' is particularly helpful. He characterizes 'collaboration' as being driven by a set of common concerns, narrowly functional, and focused strongly on looked-for gains. In such contexts, the partners in a collaborative activity are regarded as a resource or a source of information, rather than as members of a 'community of practice'. Fielding goes on to suggest that collaboration is, therefore, a plural form of individualism in which participants are typically intolerant of time spent on anything other than the task in hand. He argues that, once the task has been completed or priorities have changed, the drive behind collaboration is weakened and such collaborative working arrangements will become more tenuous, and may disappear altogether. 'Collegiality', on the other hand, is characterized as being a much more robust relationship. It is reciprocal and overridingly communal, and is rooted in shared ideals and aspirations and mutually valued social ends. Collegiality is, therefore, by definition, less reliant upon the pursuit of narrowly defined objectives or gains, but is based on a deeper commitment to exchange and development.

We have found that, in practice, instances of schools working together usually do not extend to collegial activity. Of course, it may be that collaboration is the forerunner to collegiality, and what we are seeing is groups of schools feeling their way towards more sustained and sustainable partnerships. Nor are the benefits of collaboration to be dismissed: the studies reported here show that, in many instances, stakeholders have experienced the practical benefits of collaborating, albeit in contexts where the outcomes tended to be narrowly defined. There is also evidence that, in at least some cases – the schools working together across the local authority detailed in Chapter 10 for example, or the headteachers combining their efforts for the benefit of a single school outlined in Chapter 8 – the success achieved through collaborative arrangements is leading to the development of a common language and to shared aspirations that might, in the longer term, provide a basis for collegial, urban communities.

Within school communities, more now needs to be done to strengthen collaborative activities and understandings, so that these develop towards a genuine sense of collegiality. Our view is that this will be achieved, in part, by encouraging headteachers to take on collective responsibility for the performance of all schools within a group or network. Specifically, the aim must be to develop more collegial relationships, based on a common commitment to improvement across schools, and to principles of equity and social justice. Provided heads genuinely feel that they are in control of the priorities that emerge from such a process, we would be optimistic that this could be achieved. In our discussions with heads, we find few who do not believe that the principle of collaboration with other schools is a good one, though many find the need to maximize the performance of their own schools (as measured by test results) in the short-term militates against the development of sustained collaborative relationships. It appears that the sharp, individual, accountability framework that kick-started improvement efforts in the early 1990s may now, especially in the most deprived and difficult educational contexts, pose an obstacle to the development of that sense of collective accountability for the wider school and student populations which best serves the needs of vulnerable pupils.

As we have explained, over recent years English schools have had to respond to a constant stream of innovations aimed at raising standards. In common with many other social organizations undergoing significant transformation efforts, in schools that are under pressure to improve the search is on for what Fullan (1991) describes as 'order and correctness'. He suggests that teachers searching for 'order' in times of complex social and organizational change will, inevitably, experience ambiguity regarding the direction and purposes of the change. Indeed, the search for 'order' is itself an attempt to determine what actions to take when faced with ambiguous situations – as is demonstrated in Chapters 2 and 3, where headteachers of 'failing' schools face the twin demands of providing clear direction for the staff, while simultaneously developing their capacity to play a much greater role in decision-making. Where a number of heads find themselves in similarly difficult situations, it seems that collaboration across schools can be an important source of reassurance in times of uncertainty.

It is also the case that those who can help to create a sense of common purpose in such contexts are more likely to be able to bring about change.

This may, in part at least, throw some light on what has occurred in the more successful collaborative arrangements we have described. Unusual and challenging factors, emanating as they do from both outside and inside schools, have created a sense of ambiguity. The collaborative arrangements introduced by some groups of headteachers have helped them to cope with this – for example the peer support initiatives described in Chapters 8 and 9. Further, as a result of their combined efforts, these headteachers are gradually identifying common principles around which their staffs can be drawn together, generating a new impetus for change across the whole school group.

Research suggests that such ambiguities in organizations increase the extent to which action is guided by values and ideology (see, for example, Weick 1985). Consequently, the values of 'powerful people' (in other words, those who can reduce ambiguity) greatly influence how the organization works and what it can become. Thus, those who can resolve ambiguity for themselves and for others can implant a new set of values into an organization. This has the potential to create a new set of relevancies and competencies, and, in so doing, is itself a source of innovation. In this way, ambiguity sets the scene for organizations to learn more about themselves and their environments, allowing them to emerge from their struggles and uncertainties into different and better adapted structures.

It seems, therefore, that the perspectives and skills of headteachers and other senior staff are central to an understanding of what needs to happen in order that the potential power of collaboration can be mobilized. Their visions for their schools, their beliefs about how they can foster the learning of all of their students, and their commitment to the power of interdependent learning, appear to be key influences. All of this means, of course, that replication of these processes in other schools or groups of schools will be difficult, particularly if those in charge are unwilling or unable to make fundamental changes in established beliefs and working patterns. This being the case, there is a very strong case for providing school leaders with professional development opportunities specifically focused on collaborative practice, which will support them in taking this work forward. The action learning approach, adopted by the headteachers whose activities are described in Chapter 9, provides a powerful strategy for such development activities.

Of course, the emphasis on school-level leadership within a change model grounded in the notion that a combination of robust national policies and strong school management is the surest way to increase attainment, has very significant implications for the roles of local authority staff. It means that they will have to adjust their priorities and ways of working in response to the development of collaborative arrangements that are led from within schools. And, at a time when they too are under increasing pressure to deliver improvements in results across their stocks of schools, this can lead to misunderstandings and tensions between senior staff in schools and their local authority partners.

Despite such difficulties, we cannot conceive of a way for collaboration to continue as a central element of effective school improvement strategies without some form of local coordination. As we have seen, the contributions

of local authority advisers can be significant in the development of collaborative arrangements (Chapters 7 and 10, for example, give useful pointers
as to how this can be achieved). Specifically, local authority staff can support
and challenge schools in relation to the agreed goals of collaborative activities
while headteachers share responsibility for the overall management of
improvement efforts within their schools.

We feel that this distinction sharpens understanding of the sorts of roles
that local authority staff need to take on: *not* managing and leading change,
but rather working in partnership with senior people in schools to strengthen
collaborative ways of working. In such contexts they can ensure that specific
challenges which derive from their knowledge of the bigger picture across the
authority are addressed, and also contribute to the clarity of purpose and
practical working arrangements, as well as playing an important role in the
monitoring and evaluation of progress. At the same time, they can help to
broker the sharing of resources and expertise. However, the changes in attitude and practice that this implies will be challenging to the existing thinking
of many experienced local authority staff. Consequently, they too need
professional development opportunities that will assist them in rethinking
their ways of working with and supporting schools.

In our view, national policymakers would be naive to overlook the influence of what happens at the local authority level, particularly in urban districts. As we have seen, local history, interconnections between schools and
established relationships are always important local factors, helping to shape
what happens, even when they are overlooked. Consequently, levers need to
be found, of the sort provided by the Leadership Incentive Grant, which will
be powerful in encouraging the development of interdependence among
groups of schools within districts. In this way, further progress can be made
towards a national education system that is geared to raising standards for all
students, in all schools, through the systematic orchestration and, sometimes,
the redistribution of available resources and expertise.

When considering the leadership of collaborative arrangements between
schools, there is also a need to reach out to others who have an interest in the
education of children and young people. In particular, it is important to
ensure that parents/carers, elected members, governors and local community
agencies and organizations are aware of, and feel confident about, the new
emphasis within school improvement, and the value of authentic collaboration. In this respect, the move towards the integration of support staff
from different agencies within district structures (that is occurring in some
parts of the country) is a very helpful development. Given the recent Children
Act, such moves are, of course, essential. Indeed, the structural changes that
are being introduced in response to the Every Child Matters policy provide a
potentially helpful interruption to the established flow of services within
urban areas. The aim must be to use the space that this creates to rethink and,
indeed, regroup. However, so far the indications are not altogether promising,
with representatives of the various interest groups tending to retreat within
established professional boundaries as often as they seek to form new professional alliances.

Fostering school to school collaboration

As we see most powerfully demonstrated in Chapter 10, there is evidence that school to school collaboration can add considerable value to the efforts of urban schools as they seek to develop their practices. However, this does not represent an easy option for the schools themselves, particularly in a context within which competition and choice continue to be the main drivers. There is also the problem of sustainability to consider. The examples we have presented have, for the most part, emerged as a result of schools being offered short-term incentives linked to the demonstration of collaborative planning and activity.

In February 2005 the Secretary of State for Education, Ruth Kelly, was quoted as saying:

> In the future I think cooperation will become not only the norm, it will probably be the only way of delivering a decent all-round education for all pupils... We have to get schools to operate as part of a network to deliver a fully comprehensive education.
>
> (Kampfner 2005)

But, within an education system that places emphasis on both competition and choice, why should schools choose to work together? Even where substantial incentives to collaborate are available, achieving authentic collaboration has proved a challenge requiring, as we have argued elsewhere, the surrendering of some degree of independent control in return for collective influence (Ainscow et al. 2005). However, we have also noted that, in some instances, arrangements that were initially stimulated through external incentives have been adopted by the partner schools, who have begun to use their own resources to sustain collaborative arrangements that have clearly benefited all.

We are similarly encouraged by the experiences reported in the various studies presented here. We find in these accounts ample evidence that school to school collaboration does have an enormous potential for fostering system-wide improvement, particularly in challenging urban contexts. They show how collaboration between schools can often provide an effective means of solving immediate problems such as staffing shortages; how it can have a positive impact in periods of crisis such as during the closure of a school; and how in the longer run schools working together can contribute to the raising of expectations and attainment in schools that have had a record of low achievement. There is also some evidence here that collaboration can help to reduce the polarization of schools according to their position in league tables, to the particular benefit of those students who seem marginalized at the edges of the system and whose performance and attitudes cause increasing concern. This does, of course, add support to the argument presented by Ruth Kelly.

There is evidence, too, that when schools seek to develop more collaborative ways of working, this can have an impact on how teachers perceive themselves and their work. Specifically, comparisons of practice can lead teachers to view underachieving students in a new light. Rather than simply presenting problems that are assumed to be insurmountable, such students may be perceived as providing feedback on existing classroom arrangements. In this way they may be seen as sources of understanding as to how these arrangements might be developed in ways that could be of benefit to all members of the class.

Of course, the approaches to collaboration reported in these studies vary considerably in scope and ambition, and in terms of their impact on practice and learning outcomes. Their impact ranges from the direct and short-term, to the indirect and longer term. Some strategies are essentially short-term 'fixes' aimed at immediate issues of concern (such as getting out of special measures), but with little or no potential for longer term impact. Others are intended to bring about much more fundamental changes (for example, changes in the school's culture or image), which may take several years to achieve or before any difference is noted. Many strategies fall somewhere in between (for example, coordinated local strategy for inclusion; setting up an action-learning set for headteachers), offering some combination of short-term impact and longer term development.

Looking at the accounts, it seems that activities that have a direct and immediate impact on achievement tended to be *relatively* easy to implement. Other strategies involve processes that are intended to increase the capacity of schools and their staff to develop more effective teaching and learning arrangements in response to identified needs. By their nature, these take a little longer to implement, not least because they require the negotiation of common priorities and shared values. They also require an investment of human resources in order to create a framework for management and coordination, as we saw in the account of the four schools that worked together to improve conditions in one of their number (Chapter 7). This reminds us that trust takes time to develop.

Examples such as this underline that in moving collaboration forward, from a strategy for addressing various forms of delinquency, to one that embraces and plans for the development of all schools and students within a network, the issue of shared leadership is a central driver. As we have argued, it requires the development of leadership practices that involve many stakeholders collectively sharing responsibility for improving the achievement of learners in all of the schools within a collaborative. Often this necessitates significant changes in beliefs and attitude, and new relationships as well as improvements in practice. The goal, however, must be to ensure that collaboration is between school communities and not restricted to headteachers, not least because arrangements that rely on one person are unlikely to survive the departure of those individuals who brokered them.

Using available expertise

A key to improvement in urban schools is, then, to make use of the pressure for change stemming from national policies, while mobilizing available human resources at the local level around a common sense of purpose. This is most likely to be achieved when local leadership makes connections between national policies and local priorities. It also means that there is a need to create locally the organizational conditions and climate within which stakeholders will feel encouraged to work together creatively to invent new and more effective responses to old problems – especially those of learners who are not making satisfactory progress. This requires the development of leadership that will encourage action and shared responsibility at all levels of the system. And with regard to children's learning experiences, the classroom level is crucial, since it is clear that teachers *are* decision-makers and, therefore, policymakers (Fulcher 1989). Changing policy and practice at that level is particularly difficult, however, in that it most often requires changes in thinking and beliefs.

As we have seen, at the heart of the processes in schools where changes in practice do occur, is the development of a common vocabulary in which colleagues can talk to one another about and, indeed, reflect themselves on the detail of their practice. Without such a vocabulary, teachers find it very difficult to describe in detail what they currently do and how this might be altered. Consequently, a language of classroom practice seems a prerequisite to the exploration of new possibilities. It seems that much of what teachers do during the multiple and intensive encounters that occur daily in the classroom, is carried out at an automatic, intuitive level. Furthermore, there is little time to stop and think. This is why the opportunity to see colleagues at work in the classroom is so crucial to the success of attempts to develop practice. It is through such shared experiences that colleagues can help one another to describe what they currently do and articulate what they might like to do (Hiebert et al. 2002). In essence, together they can create a language of practice. This also offers a means whereby taken for granted assumptions about particular groups of students can be revisited, challenged and subjected to mutual critique.

As we saw in Chapters 4, 7 and 9, engaging with evidence can be especially helpful in encouraging such dialogue between practitioners. Specifically, it can help to create space for reappraisal and rethinking, by interrupting existing discourses, and by focusing attention on overlooked possibilities for moving practice forward. However, the introduction of inquiry-based approaches that seek to build on existing expertise within schools is particularly difficult in challenging urban contexts. The tensions between the efforts such approaches require and the intensive pressure to achieve rapid improvements in test and examination results may discourage staff from committing themselves to what are, by their nature, improvement strategies which take time to have an impact. This is why leadership at the school level is so crucial: it must make space for such developments, despite the pressures from external scrutiny.

Moving forward

In recent years we have been privileged to work with a group of headteachers who were brought together because they had been successful in bringing about significant improvement in schools in difficult urban contexts. One project we worked on with this group involved the design of strategies that could help others to follow a similar journey of improvement in their own schools. As part of this work, we developed a framework that heads could use to identify areas of successful practice in the school, while at the same time pinpointing less effective areas where ways of working needed to be changed (Ainscow et al. 2003c).

The heads involved in this work recalled that there had been a sense of helplessness in some of their schools that had to be overcome before progress was possible. It seems that the first important achievement of these head-teachers was to move their school communities on beyond this feeling of 'helplessness' to the belief that things could and must change. Such a belief involves developing teachers' capacity to imagine what might be achieved, and increasing their sense of accountability for bringing this about. In a number of cases, it involved tackling habits, most often relating to behaviour or attendance, that had settled into norms within the school. Such habits had come to be regarded as part of the landscape, rather than things that could and should be changed. Sometimes, the change needed was within the community – parents who were happy with the school as it was, rather than seeking improvements; and families that looked to the school to improve attainment, but did not link this to their own support for the school.

What became evident was that the first step, creating the initial momentum and the self-belief among staff and students that goes with it, was seen as the most difficult to take. Though the initial achievement may have been modest in relation to what the school eventually achieved, these headteachers felt that progress became easier as the school's capacity and self-confidence increased over time. It was *knowing how to make a start* that mattered.

We concluded that the starting point, most often, must be with an analysis of the *quality of student experience* that is provided within a school. This can be thought of in terms of three interconnected dimensions:

- *Presence.* How reliably and punctually students attend school and lessons.
- *Participation.* The quality of their experiences while they are there (therefore, incorporating the views of the students themselves).
- *Achievement.* The outcomes of learning as measured by test and examination results.

At the same time, it is important to think of the way the school's resources are mobilized in relation to student experience by analysing three sets of 'arrangements' – those relating to the classroom, to management and to the wider context.

- *Classroom arrangements* are concerned with the quality of interactions between staff and students, and focus specifically on the teaching repertoires used, relationships and the support provided for learners.
- *Management arrangements* are about the way that staff and resources are deployed, and embraces leadership and staff development strategies.
- *Contextual arrangements* refer to the school's engagement with relevant stakeholders, both local (in the environment) and professional (in the system), and its links with community and external support agencies.

Drawing on research findings from school improvement and effectiveness studies, it is possible to identify factors that influence the quality of these arrangements. The presence (or absence) of these factors is likely to determine the strength of leverage that is brought to bear on student experience. Furthermore, there are factors that students can themselves contribute to the quality of their own experience.

Since it will be the way these arrangements combine with one another, and with student determined variables, that influences the quality of learning, it seems sensible to analyse for the presence or absence of these factors. Indeed, by analysing classroom, school and contextual arrangements, it is possible to see how leverage might be increased. Then, by monitoring student experience, both the impact of these levers and the influence of student related variables can be assessed.

Continuing with the search for powerful levers, then, we believe that it will be helpful to those at the local level who are encouraging schools to collaborate if national policy initiatives continue to emphasize the principle of collaboration as being a fundamental element of efforts to raise standards across the education system; and, remembering that 'what gets measured gets done', regulatory frameworks must pay due attention to this same principle. In our view this is the way *'to get schools to operate as part of a network to deliver a fully comprehensive education'*.

Clearly, then, there are implications here for the way the government develops and implements national policy. It needs to reflect on how the general increase in standards achieved over the past ten years can be spread more effectively to those areas of social and economic deprivation where the most difficult school environments are found. It needs to think carefully about how a policy framework that facilitates improvement efforts in already successful schools may hinder similar efforts in schools facing more challenging circumstances. It needs to acknowledge (because, surely, it must already understand) that strategies which have been successful for the majority of schools, have nevertheless created additional problems for the minority. Unfortunately, there is little evidence as yet that a more carefully calibrated strategy is forthcoming.

Our analysis of these studies suggests that certain types of national action can indeed be powerful in providing incentives for change and in encouraging a sense of common purpose within and between school communities. Here the role of evidence in relation to regulation seems to be a significant lever for change. Government needs to concentrate its attention on this factor and the recent changes in the Ofsted school inspection framework are encouraging in this respect. At the same time, it needs to recognize that matters of the detail of policy implementation are not amenable to central regulation. Rather, these have to be dealt with by those who are close to and, therefore, in a better position to understand local contexts. They should be trusted to act in the best interests of the children and young people they serve, and encouraged to work together, pooling their knowledge and experience, for the benefit of students and teachers alike.

Concluding remarks

We prefaced this book with a working definition of what we understand by the term 'urban education', pointing out that, while this is a relatively new term in some countries, it is one that is already established in other parts of the world. It is to this international phenomenon of difficult schools in disadvantaged areas and communities that we turn finally.

In the last few years we have been involved in school improvement projects in cities as diverse as Beijing, Bucharest, Hong Kong, Lisbon and Sao Paulo. We also have close links with fellow researchers in Australia, Canada and the USA who are engaged in similar activities. These international experiences convince us that the ideas we have explored and the conclusions we have reached in this book have relevance beyond the shores of our own country.

Throughout the world, policymakers and practitioners are faced with the challenge of underachievement among children and young people in urban contexts. And, in responding to these challenges, there is increasing evidence that collaboration within schools and between schools is seen as being the best way forward. It seems, then, that it is not only in England that there is reason to believe that *within* urban schools and their communities there is far greater potential for school improvement than is currently being utilized. Unfortunately, however, while national reform efforts have heightened the sense of urgency in relation to the challenge of urban education, they have also tended to create barriers to the sharing and creation of knowledge.

There is, therefore, a need for a major shift in overall policy direction. As we have argued in this chapter, this must involve an emphasis on forms of leadership that will foster collaboration and creativity at the local level. In this respect, the idea of school to school collaboration seems to be one that has found its moment. The evidence we have presented in this book suggests that, under certain conditions, partnerships between schools can generate powerful levers for change.

REFERENCES

Ainscow, M. (1998) Reaching out to all learners: some lessons from experience. Paper presented at the International Congress for School Effectiveness and Improvement, Manchester.

Ainscow, M. (1999) *Understanding the Development of Inclusive Schools*. London: Falmer Press.

Ainscow, M. (2000) Reaching out to all learners: some lessons from international experience, *School Effectiveness and School Improvement*, 11(1): 1–9.

Ainscow, M. (2005) Developing inclusive education systems: what are the levers for change?, *Journal of Educational Change*, 6(2): 109–24.

Ainscow, M., Barrs, D. and Martin, J. (1998) Taking school improvement into the classroom, *Improving Schools*, 1(3): 43–8.

Ainscow, M., Beresford, J., Harris, A., Hopkins, D., Southworth, G. and West, M. (2000a) *Creating the Conditions for School Improvement*, 2nd edn. London: David Fulton Publishers.

Ainscow, M., Booth, T., Dyson, A. et al. (in press) *Improving Schools, Developing Inclusion*. London: RoutledgeFalmer.

Ainscow, M. and Brown, D. (1999) (eds) *Guidance on Improving Teaching*. Lewisham: Lewisham LEA.

Ainscow, M., Farrell, P. and Tweddle, D. (2000b) Developing policies for inclusive education: a study of the role of local education authorities, *International Journal of Inclusive Education*, 4(3): 211–29.

Ainscow, M. and Fox, S. (2003) *Linking Behaviour, Learning and Leadership* (Pilot version). Manchester: National College for School Leadership with the University of Manchester.

Ainscow, M., Hargreaves, D.H. and Hopkins, D. (1995) Mapping the process of change in schools: the development of six new research techniques, *Evaluation and Research in Education*, 9(2): 75–89.

Ainscow, M., Hopkins, D., Southworth, G. and West, M. (1994) *Creating the Conditions for School Improvement*. London: Fulton.

Ainscow, M. and Howes, A. (2001) LEAs and school improvement: what is it that makes the difference? Paper presented at the British Education Research Association Conference, Leeds.

Ainscow, M., Howes, A., Farrell, P. and Frankham, J. (2003a) Making sense of the development of inclusive practices, *European Journal of Special Needs Education*, 18(2): 227–42.

Ainscow, M., Howes, A. and Tweddle, D. (2004a) Making sense of the impact of recent education policies: a study of practice, in M. Emmerich (ed.) *Public Services Under New Labour*. Manchester: Institute for Political and Economical Governance, University of Manchester.

Ainscow, M., Nicolaidou, M. and West, M. (2002) Supporting schools in difficulties: a study of the role of school-to-school cooperation. Paper presented at the BERA conference, Exeter.

Ainscow, M., Nicolaidou, M. and West, M. (2003b) Supporting schools in difficulties: the role of school-to-school cooperation, *TOPIC*, autumn (30): 1–4.

Ainscow, M. and Tweddle, D. (2003) Understanding the changing role of English local education authorities in promoting inclusion, in J. Allan (ed.) *Inclusion, Participation and Democracy: What is the Purpose?* London: Kluwer.

Ainscow, M., West, M. and Stanford, J. (2003c) *Making a New Start: A Practical Guide for Headteachers on How to Analyse Schools Causing Concern in Order to Determine Priorities for Action*. Manchester: Leadership Development Unit, University of Manchester.

Ainscow, M., West, M. and Nicolaidou, M. (2004b) Putting our heads together: a study of headteacher collaboration as a strategy for school improvement, in C. Clarke (ed.) *Improving Schools in Difficult Circumstances*. London: Continuum.

Ainscow, M., West, M., Howes, A. and Stanford, J. (2005) Why should secondary schools collaborate? An advice paper for the DfES on ways of fostering school-to-school co-operation. University of Manchester, Leadership Development Unit.

Ainscow, M., Farrell, P. and Tweddle, D. (2000) Developing policies for inclusive education: a study of the role of local education authorities, *International Journal of Inclusive Education*, 4(3): 211–29.

American Federation of Teachers (1997) *A Resource Guide for Re-Designing Low Performing Schools*. Washington: American Federation of Teachers.

Angelides, P. and Ainscow, M. (2000) Making sense of the role of culture in school improvement, *School Effectiveness and School Improvement*, 11(2): 145–64.

Ansell, D. (2004) *Improving Schools Facing Challenging Circumstances: Perspectives from Leading Thinkers*. London: NSCL, International Research Associate Perspectives.

Anyon, J. (1997) *Ghetto Schooling: A Political Economy of Urban Educational Reform*. New York: Teachers College.

Ascher, C. (1993) Changing Schools for Urban Students. The School Development Programme, accelerated Schools and Services for All. Columbia: Trends and Themes No.18, Institute for Urban and Minority Education.

Bales, R. (1952) Some uniformities of behaviour in small social systems, in G. E. Swansea, T. Newombe and E. L. Hartley (eds) *Readings in Social Psychology*. New York: Holt, Rinehart and Winston.

Bales, R. (1953) The equilibrium problem in small groups, in T. Parson, R.F. Bales and E.A. Shils (eds) *Working Papers in the Theory of Action*. Glencoe IL: Free Press.

Ball, S.J. (1997) Policy sociology and critical social research: a personal view of recent education policy and policy research, *British Educational Research Journal*, 23(1): 257–74.

Ball, S.J. (2003) *Class Strategies and the Education Market*. London: RoutledgeFalmer.

Barber, M. (1998) The dark side of the moon: imagining an end to failure in urban education, in L. Stoll and K. Myers (eds) *No Quick Fixes*. London: Falmer Press.

Bartolome, L.I. (1994) Beyond the methods fetish: towards a humanising pedagogy, *Harvard Education Review*, 54(2): 173–94.

Bass, B.M. (1997) *Transformational Leadership: Industrial, Military and Educational Impact*. London: Lawrence Erlbaum Associates.

Beatty, B.R. (2001) Emotion matters in educational leadership: an analysis of teacher-recalled interactions with administrators. Paper presented at the 82nd AERA Conference, Seattle, 10–14 April.

Bellamy, C. (1999) *The State of the World's Children: Education*. New York: UNICEF.

Benn, C. and Simon, B. (1972) *Half Way There: Report on the British Comprehensive School Reform*. Harmondsworth: Penguin Books.

Bennett, W. J. (1987) *Schools That Work: Educating Disadvantaged Children*. Washington: US Department of Education.

Bernstein, B. (1970) Education cannot compensate for society, *New Society*,

Blackstone, B. (2000) Fresh Start Schools, *Hansard*, 18 May.

Blair, T. (1997a) *PM's Parliamentary Question on Social Exclusion* – 08.12.97. London: Social Exclusion Unit.

Blair, T. (1997b) Speech by the Prime Minister on Monday 2 June at the Aylesbury Estate, Southwark. London: Social Exclusion Unit.

Blanden, J., Gregg, P. and Machin, S. (2005) *Intergeneralisation Mobility in Europe and North America*. London: Centre for Economic Performance, London School of Economics for the Sutton Trust.

Booth, T. and Ainscow, M. (2002) *The Index for Inclusion*. Bristol: Centre for Studies in Inclusive Education.

Booth, T., Ainscow, M. and Dyson, A. (1998) Inclusion and exclusion in a competitive system, in T. Booth and M. Ainscow (eds) *From Them to Us: An International Study of Inclusion in Education*. London: Routledge.

Bray, J.N., Lee, J., Smith, L.L. and Yorks, L. (2000) *Collaborative Inquiry in Action*. Thousand Oaks: Sage.

Burrell, G. and Morgan, G. (1979) *Sociological Paradigms and Organisational Analysis*. London: Heinemann.

Bush, T. and Glover, D. (2003) *School Leadership: Concepts and Evidence*. www.ncsl.org.uk/literaturereviews

Busher, H. and Hodgkinson, K. (1996) Cooperation and tension between autonomous schools: a study of inter-school networking, *Educational Review*, 48(1): 55–64.

Campbell, J., Kyriakides, L., Muijs, D. and Robinson, W. (2004) *Assessing Teacher Effectiveness*. London: RoutledgeFalmer.

Carr, W. and Kemmis, S. (1986) *Becoming Critical: Knowing Through Action Research*. London: Falmer.

Carter, S.C. (2001) *No Excuses: Lessons from 21 High Performing, High Poverty Schools*. Washington: Heritage Foundation.

Cawelti, G. (1999) *Portraits of Six Benchmark Schools: Diverse Approaches to Improving Student Performance*. New York: Education Research Service.

Centre for Studies on Inclusive Education (2000) *The Index for Inclusion: Developing Learning and Participation in Schools*. Bristol: CSIE.

Chamber, R. (1992) *Rural Appraisal: Rapid, Relaxed and Participatory*. Brighton: Institute of Development Studies.

Copland, M. A. (2003) Leadership of inquiry: building and sustaining capacity for school improvement, *Educational Evaluation and Policy Analysis*, 25(4): 375–95.

Cotton, K. (1991) Educating Urban Minority Youth: Research on Effective Practices. NWEL: School Improvement Research Series.

Crowther, D., Cummings, C., Dyson, A. and Millward, A. (2003) *Schools and Area Regeneration*. Bristol: Policy Press.

Cuckle, P. and Broadhead, P. (1999) Effects of Ofsted on school development and staff moral, in C. Cullingford (ed.) *An Inspector Calls*. London: Kogan Press.

Cummings, C., Dyson, A., Todd, L. and the Education Policy and Evaluation Unit, U.o.B (2004) *An Evaluation of the Extended Schools Pathfinder Projects*. Research Report 530. London: DfES.

Cummings, C., Dyson, A., Papps, I., Pearson, D. and Raffo, C. (2005) *Evaluation of the Full-service Extended Schools Initiative: End of First Year Report*. London: DFES.

Cutler, P. (1999) Decoration and re-construction, in L. Stoll and K. Myers (eds) *No Quick Fixes*. London: Falmer Press.

Dean, J. P. (1954) Participant observation and interviewing, in J. Doby, E.A. Sychman, J. C. McKinnet, R.G. Francis and J. P. Dean (eds) *An Introduction to Social Research*. Harrisburg, PA: Stackpole Company.

De Carvalho, M.E.P. (2001) *Rethinking Family-School Relations: A Critique of Parental Involvement in Schooling*. Mahwah, NJ: Lawrence Erlbaum Associates.

Delamont, S. (1992) *Fieldwork in Educational Settings*. London: Falmer.

Denton, J. (1998) *Organisational Learning and Effectiveness*. London: Routledge.

DfEE (Department for Education and Employment) (1997) *Excellence in Schools*, White paper. London: DfEE.

DfEE (Department for Education and Employment) (2001) *The Code of Practice on LEA–School Relations*. London: DfES.

DfES (Department for Education and Skills) (2002) *Extended Schools: Providing Opportunities and Services for All*. London: DfES.

DfES (Department for Education and Skills) (2003a) *Every Child Matters, Cm. 5860*. London: The Stationery Office.

DfES (Department for Education and Skills) (2003b) *Full-Service Extended Schools Planning Documents*. London: DfES.

DfES (Department for Education and Skills) (2004a) *Every Child Matters: Change for Children*. London: DfES.

DfES (Department for Education and Skills) (2004b) *Every Child Matters: Change for Children in Schools*. London: DfES.

DfES (Department for Education and Skills) (2004c) *Every Child Matters: Next Steps*. London: DfES.

DfES (Department for Education and Skills) (no date) *Extended Schools Detailed Guidance*. London: DfES.

Dyson, A. and Millward, A. (2000) *Schools and Special Needs: Issues of Innovation and Inclusion*. London: Paul Chapman.

Dyson, A., Millward, A. and Todd, L. (2002) *A Study of the Extended Schools Demonstration Projects*, Research Report 381. London: DfES.

Ebbutt, D. (1983) *Educational Action Research: Some General Concerns and Specific Quibbles*. Cambridge: Cambridge Institute of Education mimeo.

Edmonds, R. (1979) Effective schools for the urban poor, *Educational Leadership*, October: 15–34.

Education Trust (1999) *Dispelling the Myth: High Poverty Schools Exceeding Expectations*. London: Education Trust.

Eisner, E.W. (1988) Educational connoisseurship and criticism: their form and functions in educational evaluation, in D. Fetterman (ed.) *Educational Evaluation*.

Elbaz, F. (1991) Research on Teachers' Knowledge. Journal of Curriculum Studies. 23 (1) Reference taken from A Hargreaves. Paper presented at the Annual Meeting of the American Research Association, New Orleans, April 1994.

Elliot, J. (1981) *Action Research: A Framework for Self-evaluation in Schools*. Cambridge: Cambridge Institute of Education.

Elmore, R. (2000) *Building a New Structure for School Leadership*. Washington: The Albert Shanker Institute.

Elmore, R.F. (2004) *School Reform from the Inside Out*. Cambridge: Harvard Education Press.

Elmore, R.F., Peterson, P.L. and McCarthy, S.J. (1996) *Restructuring in the Classroom: Teaching, Learning and School Organisation*. San Francisco: Jossey-Bass.

Feinstein, L., Duckworth, K. and Sabates, R. (2004) *A Model of the Inter-generational Transmission of Educational Success*, Wider Benefits of Learning Research Report No.10. London: Centre for Research on the Wider Benefits of Learning.

Fielding, M. (1999) Radical collegiality: affirming teaching as an inclusive professional practice, *Australian Educational Researcher*, 26(2): 1–34.

Fielding, M. (2001) Target setting, policy pathology and student perspectives: learning to labour in new times, in M. Fielding (ed.) *Taking Education Really Seriously*. London: RoutledgeFalmer.

Finkelstein, N.D. and Grubb, W.N. (2000) Making sense of education and training markets: lessons from England, *American Educational Research Journal*, 37(3): 601–31.

Foster, W. (1989) Toward a critical practice of leadership, in J. Smyth (ed.) *Critical Perspectives on Educational Leadership*. London: Falmer Press.

Frankham, J. and Howes, A. (in press) Talk as action in 'collaborative action research': making and taking apart teacher/researcher relationships, *British Educational Research Journal*.

Fulcher, G. (1989) Disabling Policies? *A Comparative Approach to Education Policy and Disability*. London: Falmer.

Fullan, M. (1991) *The New Meaning of Educational Change*. London: Cassell.

Fullan, M. (2001) *Leading in a Culture of Change*. San Francisco: Jossey-Bass.

Georgiades, N.J. and Phillimore, L. (1975) The myth of the hero-innovator and alternative strategies for organisational change, in C. Kiernan and F.P. Woodford (eds) *Behaviour Modification for the Severely Retarded*. Amsterdam: Associated Scientific.

Gewirtz, S. (1998) Can all schools be successful? An exploration of the determinants of school 'success', *Oxford Review of Education*, 24(4): 439–57.

Gillborn, D. and Youdell, D. (2000) *Rationing Education: Policy, Practice, Reform and Equity*. Buckingham: Open University Press.

Gillborn, D. and Mirza, H.S. (2000) *Educational Inequality*. London: Ofsted.

Giroux, H.A. and Schmidt, M. (2004) Closing the achievement gap: a metaphor for children left behind, *Journal of Educational Change*, 5: 213–28.

Glickman, C. D. (2003) *Holding Sacred Ground: Essays on Leadership, Courage and Endurance in our Schools*. San Francisco: Jossey Bass.

Golba, A. (1998) How does education in urban schools compare to suburban schools? *www.iusb.edu/* in journal/1998/Paper5.html.

Goleman, D., Boyiatzis, R. and McKee, A. (2002) *The New Leaders: Transforming the Art of Leadership into the Science of Results*. London: Time Warner Books Ltd.

Gorard, S. (2000) *Education and Social Justice*. Cardiff: University of Wales Press.

Gray, J. (1999) *Causing Concern but Improving: A Review of Schools' Experiences*. London: DfEE.

Gray, J. and Wilcox, B. (1995) The Challenge of Turning Round Ineffective Schools, in J. Gray and B. Wilcox (eds) *Good School, Bad School*. Buckingham: Open University Press.

Gunter, H.M. (2001) *Leaders and Leadership in Education*. London: PCP.

Gunter, H.M. (2005) *Leading Teachers*. London: Continuum.

Gunter, H.M. (in press) Educational leadership and diversity, *Educational Management, Administration and Leadership*.

Hammersley, M. (1992) *What's Wrong With Ethnography?* London: Routledge.

Hardy, L. (1999) Building blocks of reform, *American School Board Journal*, February: 1–11.

Hargreaves, A. (1994) *Changing Teachers, Changing Times*. London: Cassell.

Hargreaves, D.H. (1995) School culture, school effectiveness and school improvement, *School Effectiveness and School Improvement*, 6(91): 23–46.

Hargreaves, D.H. (2003a) 'From improvement to transformation'. Keynote speech, International Congress for School Effectiveness and Improvement, Sydney, Australia.

Hargreaves, D.H. (2003b) *Education Epidemic: Transforming Secondary Schools Through Innovation Networks*. London: Demos.

Hargreaves, D.H. (2003c) Leadership for transformation within the London Challenge. Annual lecture at the London Leadership Centre, 19 May.

Hargreaves, D. and Hopkins, D. (1991) *The Empowered School*. London: Cassell.

Harris, A. (2003) The changing context of leadership: research, theory and practice, in A. Harris, C. Day, D. Hopkins, M. Hadfiled, A. Hargreaves and C. Chapman (eds) *Effective Leadership for School Improvement*. London: Routledge.

Harris, J. (2005) *So Now Who Do We Vote For?* London: Faber & Faber.

Harris, A. and Chapman, C. (2002) *Leadership in Schools in Challenging Circumstances*. Report to the National College for School Leadership.

Harris, A., Muijs, D., Chapman, C., Stoll, L. and Russ, J. (2003) *Raising Attainment in Schools in Former Coalfield Areas*, Research Report 423. London: DfES.

Hart, S. (1996) *Beyond Special Needs: Enhancing Children's Learning Through Intuitive Thinking*. London: Paul Chapman.

Hiebert, J., Gallimore, R. and Stigler, J.W. (2002) A knowledge base for the teaching profession: what would it look like and how can we get one?, *Educational Researcher*, 31(5): 3–15.

Hills, J. and Stewart, K. (2005) *A More Equal Society? New Labour, Poverty, Inequality and Exclusion*. Bristol: Policy Press.

Hitt, W. D. (1988) *The Leader Manager*. Columbus, OH: Battelle Press.

Holland, D. and Lave, J. (2001) History in person: an introduction, in D. Holland and J. Lave (eds) *History in Person*. Santa Fe, New Mexico: School of American Research Press.

Hopkins, D. (2000) Schooling for tomorrow: innovation and networks, Portuguese seminar, OECD/CERI, Lisbon.

Hopkins, D. (2001) *School Improvement for Real*. Lewes: Falmer Press.

Hopkins, D., Ainscow, M. and West, M. (1994) *School Improvement in an Era of Change*. London: Cassell.

Hoy, W. and Miskel, C. (2001) *Educational Administration: Theory, Research and Practice*. New York: McGraw-Hill.

Huberman, M. (1993) The model of the independent artisan in teachers' professional relationships, in J.W. Little and M.W. McLaughlin (eds) *Teachers' Work: Individuals, Colleagues and Contexts*. New York: Teachers College Press.

Iano, R.P. (1986) The study and development of teaching: with implications for the advancement of special education, *Remedial and Special Education*, 7(5): 50–61.

James, C. and Connolly, U. (2003) *Effective Change in Schools*. London: Routledge-Falmer.

Johnson, J. (1999) *Hope for Urban Education*. University of Austen, TX: Charles Dana Center.

Johnson, D.W. and Johnson, R.T. (1989) *Leading the Cooperative School*. Edina, MN: Interaction Book Company.

Johnson, D. W. and Johnson, R.T. (1994) *Learning Together and Alone*. Boston: Allyn and Bacon.

Kampfner, J. (2005) She has a new vision for comprehensive schools, *New Statesman*, February: 26–7.

Keddie, N. (1971) Classroom knowledge, in M.F.D. Young (ed.) *Knowledge and Control*. London: Macmillan.

Kemmis, S. and McTaggart (1982) *The Action Research Planner*. Victoria: Deakin University Press.

Keys, W., Sharp, C., Greene, K. and Grayson, H. (2003) *Successful Leadership in Urban and Challenging Contexts*. Nottingham: NCSL.

Kugelmass, J. and Ainscow, M. (2004) Leading inclusive schools: a comparison of practices in three countries, *Journal of Research in Special Needs Education*, 4(3).

Lambert, L., Walker, D., Zimmerman, D. P. et al. (1995) *The Constructivist Leader*. New York: Teachers College Press.

Lather, P. (1986) Research as praxis, *Harvard Educational Review*, 56(3): 110–29.

Lauria, M. and Mirón, J. (2005) *Urban Schools*. New York: Peter Lang Publishing.

Le Grand, J. and Bartlett, W. (eds) (1993) Quasi-Markets and Social Policy. London: Macmillan.

Leithwood, K. and Jantzi, D. (2000) The effects of transformational leadership on organisational conditions and student engagement, *Journal of Educational Administration*, 38(2): 112–29.

Leithwood, K., Jantzi, D. and Steinbach, R. (1999) *Changing Leadership for Changing Times*. Buckingham: Open University Press.

Levin, B. (2005) Thinking about improvements in schools in challenging circumstances. Paper presented at the American Educational Research Association, Montreal, April.

Levine, D.U. and Lezotte, L.W. (1990) Unusually Effective Schools: a review and analysis of research and practice. Madison WI: National Centre for Effective Schools Research and Development.

Lewin, K. (1946) Action research and minority problems, *Journal of Social Issues*, 2: 34–6.

Lingard, B., Hayes, D. and Mills, M. (2003) Teachers and productive pedagogies: contextualising, conceptualising, utilising, *Pedagogy, Culture and Society*, 11(3): 399–424.

Lipman, P. (1997) Restructuring in context: a case study of teacher participation and the dynamics of ideology, race and power, *American Educational Research Journal*, 34(1): 3–37.

Lipman, P. (2004) *High Stakes Education: Inequality, Globalisation and Urban School Reform*. New York: Routledge.

Little, J. W. and McLaughlin, M. W. (eds) (1993) *Teachers' Work: Individuals, Colleagues and Contexts*. New York: Teachers College Press.

Lloyd, C. and Payne, J. (2003) The political economy of skill and the limits of education policy, *Journal of Education Policy*, 18(1): 85–107.

Lo, M. L. (2004) *Catering for Individual Differences Through Learning Studies*. Hong Kong: Centre for the Development of School Partnership and Field Experience, Hong Kong Institute of Education.

Louis, K. S. and Miles, M. B. (1990) *Improving the Urban High School*. New York: Teachers College Press.

Lupton, R. (2004a) Do poor neighbourhoods mean poor schools?, *Education and the Neighbourhood Conference*. Bristol: Centre for Neighbourhood Research.

Lupton, R. (2004b) Schools in disadvantaged areas: recognising context and raising quality, Case paper 76. London: Centre for the Analysis of Social Exclusion, London School of Economics.

Machin, S., McNally, S. and Rajagopalan, S. (2005) *Tackling the Poverty of Opportunity: Developing 'RBS Enterprise Works' for The Prince's Trust*. London: The Prince's Trust.

McMahon, A. (2003) Fair Furlong Primary School: five years on, in M. Preedy, R. Glatter and C. Wise (eds) *Strategic Leadership and Educational Improvement*. London: Paul Chapman.

Maden, M. (2001) Further lessons in success, in M. Maden (ed.) *Success Against the Odds – Five Years On*. New York: Routledge-Falmer.

Miles, S. and Kaplan, (2005) Using images to promote reflection: an action research study in Zambia and Tanzania, *Journal of Research on Special Educational Needs*, 5(2): 77–83.

Miner, B. (1998) Reconstitution trend cools, *Rethinking Schools*, 13(2): 118–35.

Mittler, P. (2000) *Working Towards Inclusive Education*. London: Fulton.

Moore, M., Jackson, M., Fox, S. and Ainscow, M. (2004) *The Manchester Inclusion Standard*. Manchester: Manchester City Council.

Mortimer, P. and Whitty, G. (2000) Can school improvement overcome the effects of educational disadvantage?, in T. Cox (ed.) *Combating Educational Disadvantage: Meeting the Needs of Vulnerable Children*. London: Falmer Press.

Moss, P., Petrie, P. and Poland, G. (1999) *Rethinking School: Some International Perspectives*. Leicester: Youth Work Press for the Joseph Rowntree Foundation.

Muijs, D., Harris, A., Chapman, C., Stoll, L. and Russ, J. (2004) Improving schools in economically disadvantaged areas: a review of research evidence, *School Effectiveness and School Improvement*, 15(2): 149–75.

Myers, K. (1995) *Intensive care for the chronically sick*. Paper presented at the Conference for Educational Research, University of Bath.

Myers, K. (1996) *School Improvement in Practice: Schools Make a Difference Project*. London: Falmer Press.

Myers, K. and Goldstein, H. (1998) Who's Failing?, in L. Stoll and K. Myers (eds) *No Quick Fixes*. London: Falmer Press.

NCSL (2001) *Making the Difference: Successful Leadership in Challenging Circumstances*, Leading Edge Series. Nottingham: NCSL.

Nias, J., Southworth, G. and Yeomans, R. (1989) *Staff Relationships in the Primary School*. London: Cassell.

Nicolaidou, M. (2002) Understanding failing schools: perspectives from the inside. Unpublished PhD, University of Manchester.

Nicolaidou, M. (2005) What's special about special measures? Perspectives from the inside, in P. Clarke (ed.) *Improving Schools in Difficulty*. London: Continuum International Publishing Group-Academi.

Nicolaidou, M., Ainscow, M. and Howes, A. (2001) Making sense of the role of English Local Education Authorities in relation to failing schools. Paper presented at the International Congress for School Effectiveness and Improvement, Toronto, Canada.

Nicolaidou, M. and Ainscow, M. (2005) Understanding failing schools: perspectives from the inside, *School Effectiveness and School Improvement*, 16(3): 225–48.

Noddings, N. (2003) Is teaching a practice?, *Journal of Philosophy of Education*, 37(2): 241–51.

Nussbaum, M. (1999) Women and equality: the capabilities approach, *International Labour Review*, 138(3): 227–45.

Ofsted (Office for Standards in Education) (1993a) *The Handbook for the Inspection of Schools*. London: Ofsted.

Ofsted (Office for Standards in Education) (1993b) *Access and Achievement in Urban Education*. London: HMSO.

Ofsted (Office for Standards in Education) (1997) *From Failure to Success: How Special Measures are Helping Schools to Improve*. London: Ofsted.

Ofsted (2000) *Evaluating Educational Inclusion*. London: Ofsted.

Ofsted (Office for Standards in Education) (1999) Lessons Learned from Special Measures. London: The Stationery Office.

Orfield, G. (1999) Is reconstitution the answer for stuggling schools?, *The American School Board Journal*, February: 1999, 12–14.

Orfield, G. (2000) *Wrong Turn: The Trouble with Special Measures*. http://education.guardian.co.uk/print/0,3858,4039096,00.html

Phillips, R. and Harper-Jones, G. (2003) Whatever next? Education policy and New Labour: the first four years, 1997–2001, *British Educational Research Journal*, 29(1): 125–32.

Peterson, K.D. (1994) Building Collaborative Cultures, Seeking Ways to Reshape urban Schools: NCREL, U.S. Dept of Education, Office of Educational research and Improvement.

Poplin, M. and Weeres, J. (1992) *Voices From the Inside: A Report on Schooling From Inside the Classroom*. Claremont, CA: Institute for Education in Transformation.

Reason, P. (1988) *Human Inquiry in Action: Developments in New Paradigm Research*. London: Sage.

Reason, P. and Rowan, J. (1981) *Human Inquiry: A Sourcebook for New Paradigm Research*. Chichester: Wiley.

Reynolds, D. (1991) Changing ineffective schools, in M. Ainscow (eds) *Effective Schools for All*. London: Fulton.

Reynolds, D. (1995) The problem of ineffective school: some evidence and some speculations. Paper Presented at the School Effectiveness and School Improvement Seminal Series. Homerton College, Cambridge.

Reynolds, D. (1998) *The Study and Remediation of Inefective Schools: Some Further Reflections* in Stoll, L. and Myers, K. Eeds) No Quick Fixes London: Palmer Press.

Reynolds, D., Bollen, R., Creemers, B. et al. (1996) *Making Good Schools: Linking School Effectiveness and Improvement*. Oxford: Pergamon.

Reynolds, M.C. and Ainscow, M. (1994) Education of children and youth with special needs: an international perspective, in T. Husen and T.N. Postlethwaite (eds) *The International Encyclopedia of Education*, 2nd edn. Oxford: Pergamon.

Reynolds, D., Hopkins, D., Potter, D. and Chapman, C. (2002) *School Improvement for Schools Facing Challenging Circumstances: A Review of Research Practice*. London: DfES.

Riehl, C.J. (2000) The principal's role in creating inclusive schools for diverse students: a review of normative, empirical, and critical literature on the practice of educational administration, *Review of Educational Research*, 70(1): 55–81.

Robinson, V.M.J. (1998) Methodology and the research-practice gap, *Educational Researcher*, 27: 17–26.

Rosenholtz, S. (1989) *Teachers' Workplace: The Social Organisation of Schools*. New York: Longman.

Rothstein, R. (2004) *Class and Schools: Using Social Economic and Educational Reform* to *Cloak the Black–White Achievement Gap*. Washington: Economic Policy Institute.

Rozmus, K. (1998) Education reform and education quality: is reconstitution the answer?, *BYU Education and Law Journal*, 4: 103–52.

Sammons, P., Power, S., Elliot, K. et al. (2003) *New Community Schools in Scotland: Final Report*, National Evaluation of the Pilot Phase. London: Institute of Education, University of London.

Schein, E. (1985) *Organizational Culture and Leadership: A Dynamic View*. San Francisco, CA: Jossey-Bass.

Schein, E. (1992) *Organization a Culture and Leadership*, 2nd edn. San Fransisco, CA: Jossey-Bass.

Schein, E.H. (2001) Clinical inquiry/research, in P. Reason and H. Bradbury (eds) *Handbook of Action Research*. London: Sage.

Schon, D.A. (1987) *Educating the Reflective Practitioner*. San Francisco: Jossey-Bass.

Sen, A. (1999) *Development as Freedom*. Oxford: Oxford University Press.

Senge (1990) *The Fifth Discipline: The Art and Practice of the Learning Organisation*. London: Century.

Sergiovanni, T.J. (1992) *Moral leadership: Getting to the Heart of School Improvement*. San Francisco: Jossey-Bass.

Skrtic, T.M. (1991) Students with special educational needs: artifacts of the traditional curriculum, in M. Ainscow (ed.) *Effective Schools for All*. London: Fulton.

Slee, R. (2004) Inclusive education: a framework for school reform, in V. Heung and M. Ainscow (eds) *Inclusive Education: A Framework for Reform*. Hong Kong: Institute of Education.

Slee, R., Weiner, G. with Tomlinson, S. (eds) (1998) *School Effectiveness for Whom?* London: Falmer.

Smyth, J. (2005) Modernising the Australian education workplace: a case of failure to deliver for teachers of young disadvantaged adolescents, *Educational Review*, 57(2): 221–33.

Spillane, J.P., Halverson, R. and Diamond, J.B. (2001) Investigating school leadership practice, *Educational Researcher*, 30(3): 23–8.

Statistics Commission (2005) *Measuring Standards in English Primary Schools*, Statistics Commission Report No.23. London: Statistics Commission.

Stark, M. (1998) No slow fixes either: how failing schools in England are being restored to health, in L. Stoll and K. Myers (eds) *No Quick Fixes*. London: Palmer Press.

Stigler, J. W. and Hiebert, J. (1999) *The Teaching Gap*. New York: The Free Press.

Stoker, G. (2003) *Public Value Management: A New Resolution of the Democracy/ Efficency Trade Off*. www.ipeg.org.uk/publications.htm

Stoll, L. and Myers, K. (eds) (1998) *No Quick Fixes*. London: Palmer Press.

Strathern, M. (2000) The tyranny of transparency, *British Educational Research Journal*, 26(3): 309–21.

Stringfield, S. (1998) An anatomy of ineffectiveness, in L. Stoll and K. Myers (eds) *No Quick Fixes*. London: Falmer Press.

Stringfield, S. Millsap, M.A., Winfield, L., Brigham, N., Yoder, N., Moss, M.,Nesselrodt, P., Schaffer, E., Bedinger, S. and Ganse, B. (1997) *Special Strategies Studies Final Report*. Washington: US Education Department.

Teddlie, C. and Reynolds, D. (eds) (2000) *The International Handbook of School Effectiveness Research*. London: Falmer Press.

Thrupp, M. (1999) *Schools Making a Difference: Let's be realistic!* Buckingham: Open University Press.

Thrupp, M. (2001a) School quasi-markets in England and Wales: Best understood as a class strategy? Paper presented at the British Educational Research Association annual conference, Leeds.

Thrupp, M. (2001b) Recent school effectiveness counter-critiques: problems and possibilities, *British Educational Research Journal*, 27(4): 443–57.

Timperley, S.H. and Robinson, V.M.J. (2001) Achieving school improvement through challenging and changing teachers' schema, *Journal of Educational Change*, 2: 281–300.

Tobin, J. (2005) Scaling up as catachresis, *International Journal of Research & Method in Education*, 28(1): 23–32.

Trent, S.C., Artiles, A.J. and Englert, C.S. (1998) From deficit thinking to social constructivism: a review of theory, research and practice in special education, *Review of Research in Education*, 23: 277–307.

Tymms, P. (2001) *Standards Over Time: Why the Key Stage Tests Cannot Monitor Standards Over Time and Why We Must Become a Learning Society*. Durham: CEM Centre.

Tymms, P. (2004) Are standards rising in English primary schools?, *British Educational Research Journal*, 30(4): 477–94.

UNESCO (2001) *The Open File on Inclusive Education*. Paris: UNESCO.

US Dept of Education (1998) *Turning Around Low-Performing Schools: A Guide for State and Local Leaders*. Washington: Department Of Education.

Vangen, S. and Huxham, C. (2003) Nurturing collaborative relations: building trust in interorganizational collaboration, *Journal of Applied Behavioral Science*, 39(1): 5–31.

Vitello, S. J. and Mithaug, D. E. (eds) (1998) *Inclusive Schooling: National and International Perspectives*. Mahwah, NJ: Lawrence Erlbaum.

Wagner, J. (1997) The unavoidable intervention of educational research: a framework for reconsidering researcher-practitioner cooperation, *Educational Researcher*, October: 13–22.

Wallace, M. (2002) Modelling distributed leadership and management effectiveness: primary school senior management teams in England and Wales, *School Effectiveness and School Improvement*, 13(2): 163–86.

Waller, W. (1932) *The Sociology of Teaching*. New York: Wiley

Wasser, J.D. and Bresler, L. (1996) Working in a collaborative zone: conceptualising collaboration in qualitative research teams, *Educational Researcher*, 25(5): 5–15.

Weick, K. E. (1976) Educational organisations as loosely coupled systems, Administrative Science Quarterly, 21: 1–19.

Weick, K. E. (1985) Sources of order in underorganised systems: themes in recent organisational theory, in Y. S. Lincoln (ed.) *Organisational Theory and Inquiry*. Beverley Hills: Sage.

Wenger, E. (1998) *Communities of Practice: Learning, Meaning and Identity*. Cambridge: Cambridge University Press.

West, M., Ainscow, M. and Nicolaidou, M. (2003) Putting our heads together. Paper at the International Congress for School Effectiveness and Improvement, Sydney, Australia.

West, M., Ainscow, M. and Notman, H. (2003) *What Leaders Read 2: Key Texts from Education and Beyond*. Nottingham: National College for School Leadership.

West, M., Ainscow, M. and Stanford, J. (2005) Sustaining improvement in schools in challenging circumstances: a study of successful practice, *School Leadership and Management*, 25(1): 77–93.

Wilkin, A., White, R. and Kinder, K. (2003) *Towards Extended Schools: A Literature Review*. London: DfES.

Winkley, D. (1999) An examination of Ofsted, in C. Cullingford (ed.) *An Inspector Calls*. London: Kogan Page.

Wohlstetter, P., Malloy, C. L. et al. (2003) Improving schools through networks: a new approach to urban school reform, *Educational Policy*, 17(4): 399–430.

Young, L.J. and Melnick, S.L. (1988) 'Forsaken Lives, Abandoned Dreams: What will compel us to act?' *Harvard Educational Review* 58/3, pp.380–394.

INDEX